NOTES ON BEETHOVEN

NOTES ON BEETHOVEN

20 Crucial Works

Conrad Wilson

William B. Eerdmans Publishing Company
Grand Rapids, Michigan

To Micaela, aged 5, who loves the 'Pastoral'

© 2003 Conrad Wilson

First published 2003 by Saint Andrew Press, Edinburgh

This edition published 2005
in the United States of America by
Wm. B. Eerdmans Publishing Company
255 Jefferson Ave. S.E., Grand Rapids, Michigan 49503

Printed in the United States of America

10 09 08 07 06 05   7 6 5 4 3 2 1

ISBN 0–8028–2930–9

www.eerdmans.com

CONTENTS

FOREWORD

Why twenty? Obviously it is a device, one way of drawing attention to some of the masterpieces in a great composer's output. But at the same time it is a discipline and a challenge. Why choose these particular works and not others? The question and its answers are my reason for writing this book and its companions on other composers. In making my selection, I thought twenty works to be a good, sufficiently tight number. Increase it to thirty and choice becomes easier, perhaps too easy. Reduce it to ten and, in the case of great productive composers, you don't really have enough music wholly to justify what you are doing. Too many crucial works would have to be excluded, and the gaps would be glaring. So twenty it is, though not in the sense of a top twenty, because a crucial work does not actually have to be a great one, and the works are not listed – how could they be? – in any order of merit.

But each of them, it seems to me, needs to mark a special moment in its composer's life – perhaps a turning point, perhaps a sudden flash of inspiration, perhaps an intensifying of genius, as when Schubert produced his setting of Goethe's 'Gretchen am Spinnrade' at the age of 17, or Mozart his G major Violin Concerto, K216, at 19, or Beethoven his C minor Piano Trio, Op. 1, No. 3, at 25.

None of these composers was a prodigy as gifted as Mendelssohn, whose String Octet and whose *A Midsummer Night's Dream* overture were the most astounding teenage masterpieces of all time. But if there was nothing so arresting to be found among Mozart's or Schubert's numerous boyhood works, the change when it came was startling.

With Schubert's first great song, Mozart's first great concerto and Beethoven's first great piece of chamber music came the shock of surprise in the form of an audacious new command of melody and accompaniment, a conspicuous leap in quality and, in the slow movement of the Mozart, a grasp of the mystery of beauty which made his two previous violin concertos, written in the same year, seem blandly impersonal exercises in composition.

Yet this third of Mozart's five violin concertos is not a masterpiece in the sense that *Don Giovanni* is, just as Schubert's boyhood String Quartet in E flat major, D87, for all its melodic beauty, is not as overwhelming as 'Death and the Maiden'. Nor, for that matter, does Beethoven's Second Symphony possess the size and sustaining power of his Third, the 'Eroica', though it has unquestionable excitements of its own.

It is not the aim of these books to set one masterpiece against another, or to suggest that early works are automatically less interesting than late ones. To regard a composer's output purely as a process of evolution is to fail inexcusably to accept a work on its own terms – a serious flaw in assessments of Schubert, who, according to many a pundit, did not 'find' himself until he was almost dead.

So, early works are not being banned from these pages, even if it means the loss of some late ones. Nor is my decision to deal with the music chronologically based on any intrinsic belief that it reflects in some special way a composer's progress. The intention is simply to shed light on what was happening to him at the time he wrote a particular piece, where he was, what he was doing or experiencing, and how the music fits into the general pattern of his life and output. To go beyond this, by claiming that Haydn, for example, 'progressed' from his *Storm and Stress* symphonies to his *London* ones, or Mozart from his E flat major Piano Concerto, K271, to his E flat major, K482, is to undervalue his achievement as a whole.

So, no masterpiece has been omitted simply because its composer later in some way surpassed it. Some works are included simply because I adore them, or am prepared to defend them against the judgement of people who detest them. Liking a piece of music, we should always remember, is not the opposite of disliking it. It is a different condition altogether, and being able to explain why we like it is perhaps more important in the end than pronouncing on whether it is good music or bad.

Each of these twenty short essays is a species of what are traditionally known as programme notes – the descriptions to be found in printed concert or opera programmes of what is being performed that night. Donald Francis Tovey, one-time professor of music at Edinburgh University, was a famed and erudite pioneer of the form in the early twentieth century, and his collected *Essays in Musical Analysis* remain good to read, even if their style now seems old-fashioned and out of tune with today's musical thinking. Nor are they always accurate. Scholarship has progressed since Tovey's time.

Nevertheless, what Tovey wrote still towers over much of what passes for programme notes today. Even during my own post-Tovey boyhood, programme notes incorporated – as Tovey's did – musical examples because it was assumed that concert-goers could read music. Today, such notes would be branded elitist. To include musical terminology at all tends to be frowned upon. I have been asked why, in my own notes, I employ such terms as 'counterpoint', which nobody understands. But are football correspondents similarly chided for writing 'penalty' or 'free kick'? Somehow I think not. Though I am all against jargon, the use of an established, accessible musical term is preferable to a paragraph of explanation.

Concert programmes are now a dumbed-down art in which fatuous puffs about the performers occupy more space than the notes themselves, and adverts are given more space still. Traditional notes, as the chief executive of a concert organisation has remarked to me, are now 'irrelevant'. In the sense that most concerts today take place in darkened halls, he was perhaps right. But notes are written to be read before and after an event, as well as during it, and this book's intention is to fill that need.

In the sixteen years I spent editing the Edinburgh Festival's programme notes, there were a number of house rules which I worked out with the then Festival director, Peter Diamand, whose European outlook differed from, and was refreshingly less 'commercial' than, the British. Diamand's beliefs, which I shared, were that notes should contain facts rather than flimflam; that speculation was acceptable so long as it was informed; that notes should be coherently devised by a single writer for the contents of a single programme; that connections between one work and another should be mentioned; that the author, as Tovey once decreed, should act as counsel for the defence – Diamand detested notes which gave the impression that 'This is a bad work but let's perform it anyway'; and that artists' biographies should be confined to 150 words, should include no adjectives and should supply no information about what a performer would be performing in future seasons.

Though most of these principles have fallen by the wayside, they are still the ones to which I, as a note-writer, would prefer to adhere. In addition, I would say that, wherever possible, a work's place in musical history needs to be established; that its local connections (if any) should be mentioned; and that the writer has a responsibility to lure the reader into the music.

Some of the notes included in these pages are based on notes originally written for one musical organisation or another, but which have gone through a constant process of change, and which have now been changed yet again to suit the needs of a book about a single great composer. No note, whether for a concert programme or for something more permanent, should be merely 'drawn from stock'. Just as every performance of a work forms a part (however small) of that work's history, so every programme note should reflect the state – and status – of that work at the time the annotator is writing about it. Attitudes alter. Here, in this book, are twenty current attitudes (my own, but also quoting those of others) to twenty works that continue to matter.

Finally, a note on format. Each book begins with a fresh assessment of its subject composer and of the way he is performed at the start of the twenty-first century. Books are listed for further reading, and technical terms are explained in a brief glossary. Recordings are recommended at the end of each short essay, with record numbers provided wherever possible. Since prices vary from shop to shop, it seems sensible simply to generalise, saying where a disc, or set of discs, is bargain-price or otherwise at the time of going to press.

CONRAD WILSON
Edinburgh, 2003

INTRODUCTION

Beethoven was born in 1770 in Bonn, John Le Carré's 'Small Town in Germany', a place dismissed for its provincial dullness when it became the seat of Konrad Adenauer's West German government after the Second World War. Sauntering along the Rhine, you may pause to tour the Beethoven house, but not for long. It is not much more interesting than Bonn itself, from which the unhappy young Beethoven escaped as soon as he could. The house has no association with the music that mattered. By the time Beethoven wrote it, he had moved to Vienna.

Though Cologne, where he was appointed deputy court organist at the age of 14, was just a few miles downstream, Beethoven's ambitions already lay further afield. This was not surprising, because his father, though also a musician, was a drunken bully, and his mother kept herself to herself. But if his father's attitude to him was strictly pedagogic – and strictly was the operative word – at least he was in no danger of being paraded round Europe as a child prodigy, as Mozart had been. He was not that sort of child, though his potential as an improviser, upon which such trips depended, was there to be exploited.

Significantly, however, it was Beethoven himself who exploited it, just as it was Beethoven himself who raised the cash to visit Vienna at the age of 16 in the hope of persuading Mozart to give him lessons. Of an actual meeting with Mozart, there is not a shred of evidence outside the realms of romantic biography. But he did, or so it seems, hear Mozart play, and complained of the 'choppiness' of his style – a description which has to be matched against Mozart's own statement that his piano music was meant to 'flow like oil'. Yet Beethoven may well have been right. Mozart, for all his youthfulness, already had such crookedly arthritic fingers that observers remarked on his inability to cut his meat. If Beethoven had been able to prolong his stay in Vienna, he would surely have met Mozart in the end. But a summons home to his mother's deathbed prevented his perseverance from being put to the test.

Haydn, passing through Bonn on his way to London three years later, whetted Beethoven's appetite once more for the Austrian capital. What they said to each other when they met on Christmas Day 1790 can only be guessed at. They may have said nothing at all, Beethoven being just one of several Bonn musicians introduced to the visiting celebrity. But when Beethoven next set out for Vienna, on 2 November 1792, it was, as his friend Count Waldstein deftly put it, 'to receive the spirit of Mozart at the hands of Haydn'. The future dedicatee of the *Waldstein* sonata, who was one of Beethoven's first patrons in Bonn, was only 30 years old at the time, but his words have gone down in history and he was soon to follow Beethoven to Vienna.

What Beethoven received at Haydn's hands was a bit of tuition which seems not to have greatly pleased either of them. What he received from Vienna was something he would never have got in Bonn: inspirational encouragement of a sort which, within a few years, set him on course to produce the greatest, most vanguard symphonies, concertos, sonatas, trios and quartets of his time. He would never live anywhere else, though he was greatly attracted to Paris; and he would never return to Bonn.

By the time he died, at the age of 57, he was considered an old man; and, by the standards of his time, that was what he was. He had been deaf, and then deafer, for quarter of a century. He had endured near-fatal illness, which inspired his A minor String Quartet, Op. 132, and the vast hymn of thanksgiving to God which formed its slow movement. He had been a gruff, scruffy, solitary yet prosperous man, who had had at least one secret love affair with someone whom he called his 'Immortal Beloved', now identified as Antonie Brentano, a married woman who eventually moved from Vienna to Frankfurt with her husband and family, leaving Beethoven bereft and, for a while, almost unable to compose.

Though his famous letter to her apparently remained undelivered, at least he never destroyed what may, in fact, have been a draft of a letter he did send. She, for her part, wrote to a certain Bishop Sailer in 1819, seven years after her departure for Frankfurt, imploring him to help Beethoven's troubled nephew Karl. In that letter, as the composer's latest, greatly perceptive biographer, Lewis Lockwood, has quoted, she described Beethoven as not only a man of 'soft heart' and 'glowing soul' but also 'greater as a human being than as an artist'. Nobody else spoke thus about him. Indeed, for most of his acquaintances, the human being was the price that had to be paid for the artist. Antonie Brentano knew better than that and, in Lockwood's words, 'could characterise him with unusual insight'.

The aftermath of the Brentano affair was poignant for a man as lonely as Beethoven, who longed for 'conjugal love' in the *Fidelio* sense but could never attain it. It is surely significant that his final rewriting of his solitary opera took place at that time. Yet, as with his bitter battle for the custody of his nephew Karl, this spell of unrest and unhappiness did not result in invariably poignant music. *Fidelio* has a happy ending. The Eighth Symphony, one of the most explosively good-humoured of all his works, showed that what he composed was not necessarily a reflection of his private feelings.

What these moments in his output did result in was the gradual dissolution of his so-called heroic, deafness-defying middle period, whose robustness of style was now moving towards the more inward, philosophical works of his final phase. The fact that his output dwindled during these years of high but private emotion was part of the process of change.

Yet dividing his works into periods has always been a misleading, if convenient, way of dealing with them, resulting in the uncomfortable forcing of some of them into the wrong mould. Today, this pigeon-holing has begun to be frowned upon, because it so often gives a false impression of his progress as a composer. Not all the music of his last period was inward. Some of his middle-period slow movements were very inward indeed. A cut-and-dried approach to Beethoven is always risky, nowhere more so than at the established cut-off points between one period and the next.

Indeed, our whole approach to him is changing, and surely for the better. The gradual grabbing of his symphonies, concertos and overtures by high-profile chamber orchestras has alarmed and dismayed the big symphony orchestras, whose exclusive terrain these works used to be. To hear them performed by the Chamber Orchestra of Europe, Scottish Chamber Orchestra, London Classical Players, or Orchestra of the Age of Enlightenment is to recognise that, with the right conductors in charge, a revolution in Beethoven performance practice has been taking place, and the results are revelatory.

If the traditional symphony orchestras are under threat, this is only what they deserve, unless they adjust themselves to change, as the Berlin Philharmonic is already doing with Sir Simon Rattle, and the Philharmonia Orchestra in its occasional appearances with Sir Roger Norrington. Sir John Eliot Gardiner's creation of his aptly named Orchestre Révolutionnaire et Romantique has had its desired shock effect, but the speed with which more conventional chamber orchestras have followed suit has been a force for good. Mixing modern instruments with period ones, Sir Charles Mackerras has imposed the best of both worlds on the Scottish Chamber Orchestra, with results which are exhilarating, incisive, stylish and properly scaled to the music.

NOTES ON BEETHOVEN

Nikolaus Harnoncourt, working with the young, modern, alert instrumentalists of the Chamber Orchestra of Europe, has been similarly successful, declaring it to be his conviction that 'music is not there to soothe people's nerves, but to open their eyes, give them a good shaking, even to frighten them'. It is an approach so in keeping with Beethoven that its rightness can hardly be disputed. David Zinman and the Zurich Tonhalle Orchestra, employing Jonathan Del Mar's accurate new edition of the symphonies and following as far as possible Beethoven's own racy metronome markings, is someone else who has recognised the need for change. Now that the old era of self-consciously 'great' Beethoven conducting has died out, and with it the extremes of the heroic, heavyweight approach to the composer, these fleet, slimmed-down, illuminating performances, with their sharper rhythms and phrasing, are greatly refreshing and convincing.

In the course of the twenty-first century, we shall recognise that the truth about Beethoven's music no longer depends on 'great' conductors but on other priorities altogether. Among these will be a general reduction in the use of vibrato, which was superimposed on orchestral tone long after Beethoven's death. Along with this, there will be increasing recognition that the bunching of all the violins on one side of the platform in the interests of glossy sound is historical malpractice. Beethoven does not need it any more than do Haydn, Mozart, Schubert or Brahms.

Yet big traditional symphony orchestras are in no danger of extinction if someone as persuasive as Sir Simon Rattle can get his hands on them. His complete recording of the symphonies with the Vienna Philharmonic, issued in April 2003 by EMI (7243 5 57445 2 4), shows how a progressive mind can work miracles with the most notoriously conservative of musicians and can get them to play Beethoven in a different way.

If the result remains a compromise, it is nevertheless an enthralling one. The new Beethoven edition is employed as a vehicle not for hair-raising speeds but for bringing higher, keener profile to the glowing tone of the great orchestra. Rattle claims Beethoven's symphonies to be musical autobiographies, just like Mahler's; and, in the juxtaposition of the Fifth and Sixth symphonies, in particular, he provides impressive support for his belief. By critical modern standards, the sound may be too big for the music – a double-sized woodwind section is heard in the Ninth Symphony in the old Karajan manner – yet the effect is never bland or grandiose. At the other end of the range, the Second Symphony emerges as a genuinely revolutionary work, in some ways the most revolutionary of them all. Performances such as these remind us that Beethoven's symphonies, like Mozart's comedies, Wagner's *Ring*, Bach's *Goldberg Variations*, and all other masterpieces of their kind, are constantly self-renewing.

One

1795
Piano Trio in C minor, Op. 1, No. 3

Allegro con brio   Adagio cantabile con variazione

Menuetto: Quasi allegro   Finale: Prestissimo

'This is the man who is to console us for the loss of Mozart', declared J. B. Cramer, the English composer and publisher, when he heard Beethoven's three piano trios, Op. 1, at Tompkinson's piano studios in London in the 1790s. As for Beethoven himself, he wrote the following words in his sketchbook during the same period: 'Here I am, 25 years old. This year must bring out the complete man – nothing must remain over.'

The complete man completed his official Opus One between the years 1792 and 1795, scrapping a previous Opus One (a set of *Marriage of Figaro* variations) to make way for the three new pieces. When he started work on them, he was still an apprentice composer in provincial Bonn, his home town on the river Rhine, yet had been active enough to have produced plenty of potential 'opus ones'. By the time he finished the three works – in those days it was considered good marketing practice to produce trios and quartets in portfolios of three or six – he had moved to Vienna to seek fame as a pianist and to become Haydn's pupil as a composer.

Fame was easily won. Haydn, by then in his sixties, proved harder. Not only was he unenthusiastic about the trios when Beethoven showed them to him, but (according to Beethoven) he severely criticised the third of them, advising against trying to have it published. Beethoven, already up to speed in dealing with publishers, ignored the advice and, as things turned out, was right to do so. Haydn, having judged young Beethoven to be too impulsive, and perhaps too uncouth, later explained that he was merely counselling caution.

The music, as we can now see, had a dynamism that must have seemed shocking even to someone as adventurous as Haydn in 1795, but which made the C minor Trio an instant and audacious success. The first movement, with its shooting scales, abrupt swings between soft and loud tone, startling modulations and ferocious vehemence, packed a punch more powerful than anything else of its kind written in Vienna up to that time. It made Haydn's and Mozart's piano trios – and Haydn in 1795 was still writing piano trios – seem, for all their beauty, to belong to a different, distant world. It provided a vivid glimpse of Beethoven striding in C minor towards the nineteenth century, and towards his sensational Symphony

No. 5 in the same key. For Beethoven in 1795, the eighteenth century was over.

Yet the slow movement, though calmer and seemingly more orthodox, is no less striking. It could be called a traditional theme and (five) variations – but the utterly Beethovenian theme is more memorable than many of its kind, and the variations are filled with genuine variety. Far from merely decorating the theme, Beethoven submits it to eloquent transformation, at different speeds, in different keys and with productive use of the cello, which, in Haydn's and Mozart's trios, had served as little more than a passenger.

The inclusion of a minuet, too, was something new, Haydn and Mozart having favoured a three-movement (even a two-movement) format for their piano trios. Yet there is nothing very minuet-like about Beethoven's minuet, a serious, rather broody movement in the minor, with an exquisite major-key trio section, filled with featherweight scales.

The finale is all lightning flashes and thunderclaps, designed to be performed as fast as possible. But what really blows through this music is a wind of change. Not only is it rhythmically more impetuous than anything previously written for piano, violin and cello, but it is studded with deliberate harmonic shock-effects – even listeners with a weak sense of pitch are bound to notice the sudden sidestep into B minor in the coda. The soft ending is usually described as 'another departure from convention'.

It is moreover, at the close of so tempestuous a movement, gloriously and dramatically right.

From his Opus One onwards, Beethoven continued boldly in the way he intended. He was not the sort of composer who, having reached the brink, stepped back – as Richard Strauss and Serge Prokofiev were later to do – and he proved it in such works as his Third, Fifth and Ninth symphonies, the 'Emperor' concerto, the 'Appassionata' and *Hammerklavier* piano sonatas, the late string quartets, the *Missa Solemnis* and the opera *Fidelio*.

After the three early, strikingly contrasted and arresting piano trios, Beethoven composed three other such works at a later stage in his life, as well as a number of shorter pieces for the same instruments. Among these, the 'Archduke' is the grandest and most famous, the 'Ghost' the most startling. Once Beethoven got his hands on it, the art of the piano trio was no longer a matter of writing a piano solo and decorating it with the sound of two less assertive instruments. Whatever the problems of the form – and the question of balance between piano and strings continues to exist – Beethoven emancipated it, leaving his successors to accept the challenge. The trios of Schubert, Schumann, Mendelssohn, Brahms, Tchaikovsky and, more recently, Alexander Goehr and Martin Dalby show how they responded.

Though record-buyers are faced with a galaxy of starry performances of this work, it can take more than big names to shed the right sort of light on music so explosive yet intimate. The Beaux Arts Trio does not need a Vladimir Ashkenazy as pianist, an Isaac Stern as violinist or a Jacqueline Du Pré as cellist. It is the group – and the group-name – that counts, defining the quality of the performance and giving it an unmatched rapport which, after more than twenty years, remains exemplary. Textures are beautifully integrated yet luminously clear. The performance sounds seasoned yet utterly alive.

The only snag is that, in order to buy the one Beethoven trio, you have to buy all the others plus a variety of odds and ends. But this is hardly a hardship, considering the quality of the music and the bargain price at which the five-disc set is available (Philips 468 411-2). If, however, price really counts, then the fascinatingly balanced performance of the three Opus One trios by Patrick Cohen, Erich Hobarth and Christopher Coin on original instruments would be the one to go for (Harmonia Mundi 1901361).

NOTES ON BEETHOVEN

Beethoven's sixteen string quartets, like his thirty-two piano sonatas, fall neatly — though not too conveniently — into three periods of his life. The first six are clear-cut early works, and thus usually identified as his 'early' quartets. The next three, bigger and more passionately ambitious, with many assertive, more experimental features, belong to his 'middle' period, as do the bigger, bolder piano sonatas.

Then come two works which rather break the pattern, falling so awkwardly between the middle and late periods that they seem to demand a separate category of their own. The final five works do have a category of their own, and that category is 'late'. By then, the music had reached a state which could be called timeless and philosophical, transcending Beethoven's now total deafness and the chaos of his personal life. Yet, once again, the first and last of these works do not quite fit the pattern. The first, Opus 127, has links with Opus 74 and Opus 95. The last disentangles itself from the preceding three works, and strides off into the future — except that, in quartet terms, there was no future.

So, in the end, Beethoven left us tantalised with a great, considerably shorter, still somewhat underrated work whose finale, in words (written in the score) and in rhythm, three times brusquely asks the question 'Must it be?' and three times supplies its own answer: 'It must be.' Many performers, by omitting an important repeated section which Beethoven took pains to include, reduce the number of times to two. In so doing, presumably through fear of boring either themselves or the audience, they brutally disturb the balance of the movement.

Two

1799
STRING QUARTET IN F MAJOR, OP. 18, No. 1

Allegro con brio

Scherzo: Allegro molto

Adagio affettuoso ed appassionato

Allegro

In the time of Haydn and Mozart, when composers were expected to be prolific, it was customary to produce string quartets in sets of six. Beethoven's Opus 18, his first published quartets, followed this practice. His next set, Opus 59, halved the quantity but substantially increased the length of each work. Thereafter, he numbered his quartets separately, though three of his last works – Op. 130, 131 and 132 – are more closely unified than any of those forming Opus 18.

What unifies the early quartets is simply their classicism, though it is a classicism already placed under threat by the force of Beethoven's powerful musical personality. The writing is lithe and aphoristic, with abrupt switches between soft and loud, violent changes of key, unexpectedly volatile scale passages, dramatic use of all four instruments, and, in the slow movement of this work, a plunge into melancholy so sombre that it prompted Beethoven's friend, Karl Ferdinand Amenda, to inform posterity that it represented the tomb scene in *Romeo and Juliet*.

Though published as No. 1, the F major was in fact the second of the set to be written. But its opening movement – even its opening motif – is enough to show why Beethoven decided to give this work pride of place in his set of six. The motif, indeed, is the movement. It is terse, neatly clinched, punctuated by pauses, and heard as many as twenty-five times in the first fifty bars. It also fills the movement's central development section – and in the end, not unpredictably, it brings the music back to where it started. Yet, for all its apparent spontaneity, this little motif cost Beethoven much trouble, and his sketchbooks show that he wrote nine different versions of it before he was satisfied. A trilling secondary theme, with an offbeat rhythm, provides contrast, along with a number of shooting scale passages; but these are mere diversions in the monothematic impulse of the movement as a whole.

In the passionate and quite large-scale adagio, the Romeo and Juliet connection is hard to ignore, even though we do not have Beethoven's personal confirmation of it. But he did know Shakespeare's play, and the atmosphere of the movement is that of an operatic scena, nocturnal and Italianate, with the first violin, joined later by the cello, singing a *bel canto* lament over a softly pulsating accompaniment. The music seems graphic, sometimes strikingly so – as when, after a sudden climax, the flow is broken by bare, detached chords growing progressively softer. But tension builds up again, and the first violin's plaintive song resumes.

After this expansive adagio, the scherzo sounds particularly pithy, the phrases short, with contrasts between rough and smooth, little trills, sudden accents and a humorous jerkiness of movement that increases in the trio section. The finale provides more of the same, its momentum brilliantly sustained, especially by the hard-working first violin, who leads the other players through some remote keys before bringing the music energetically back to base.

Before choosing a recording of this or any other Beethoven quartet, buyers should bear in mind that single discs do not always work out to financial advantage. A recent recording of the first three works of Opus 18 by 'The Lindsays', as Manchester's Lindsay Quartet is now fashionably known, is very fine, quite broadly yet vitally played. The performances, as they should, look ahead to Beethoven's middle period, rather than backwards to Haydn and Mozart (ASV CDDCA 1111).

But recommending this disc requires the proviso that this is an expensive way of acquiring these three works. New York's long-established Juilliard Quartet does all six of them more cheaply in a three-disc box. The performances, though older, have plenty of presence, and have the spontaneity – and risk factor – of having been recorded live, though Sony's liner notes reprehensibly do not say where or when. Only the names of the players, who have changed over the years, provide a clue (Sony SB3K89895).

Two further bargain-price three-disc boxes, of the middle and late quartets, complete this enthrallingly unified Juilliard cycle, notable among other things for its grandly sonorous slow movements. All Beethoven's vital repeated sections, of particular structural importance in the case of Op. 59, No. 2 and Op. 135, are included. A further Juilliard set, incorporating all sixteen quartets in an eight-disc box, is even more of a bargain, but marred by the omission of repeats.

Three

1801
SONATA IN C SHARP MINOR, OP. 27, NO. 2 ('MOONLIGHT')

Adagio sostenuto – Allegretto Presto agitato

'I generally have some pictures in my mind while composing', Beethoven once remarked – a rash statement, perhaps, when you consider the aptitude of publicists, publishers and people in general to apply scenarios to music when nothing visual was ever intended. Beethoven's Piano Sonata in C sharp minor has been identified with one indelible picture from the moment it was published, but it was not Beethoven himself who called the piece the 'Moonlight'.

Piano sonatas were among the works with which he made his first impact on Vienna, as soon as he arrived there from provincial Bonn at the age of 21. Haydn, who had passed through Bonn en route to London the previous year, and encountering the young composer again on his way home, clearly influenced Beethoven's decision to move to Vienna rather than Paris, the other city upon which he could be said to have had designs. As a gifted pianist, soon to become – though all too briefly – the greatest in Europe, Beethoven chose the piano as the primary vehicle for his inspiration and startled Viennese listeners with the audacity of his music and the way he played it.

The difference between a Mozart sonata and a Beethoven one must have been immediately apparent. Even in the earliest works, there was a new, emphatic, volatile quality about the fast movements, a new romance and pathos about the slow ones, quite foreign to previous composers, though Haydn had found his own starkly Haydnish equivalents of these things in the symphonies of his 'storm-and-stress' period. Mozart, while he could produce the pearly, moonlit beauty of the slow movement of the concerto now known as the *Elvira Madigan*, could not have written any part of the 'Moonlight' sonata.

Yet in theory, had he lived a little longer, Mozart might have gone in that direction. Though Beethoven considered the 'Moonlight' sufficiently different from his previous sonatas to call it (along with its immediate predecessor, Op. 27, No. 1, in E flat major) a *sonata quasi una fantasia*, the link between fantasy and sonata was something perfectly familiar to Mozart. Indeed, he had composed one powerfully dramatic example of such a work himself, the dual Fantasy and Sonata in C minor, K475 and 457, whose only snag is that its two halves should never be played as an entity – they simply cancel each other out, as the pianist Artur Schnabel was perhaps the first to proclaim. Beethoven's achievement in the 'Moonlight' was to merge fantasy and sonata into a unity, greatly to the work's advantage, and in doing so he paved the way for the compressed sonata-like format of Schubert's *Wanderer Fantasy*. Moreover, the strange, slow opening movement, which provides the main element of fantasy in Beethoven's sonata, is nocturnal enough to make the nickname by which generations of music-lovers have known it seem as apt as Beethoven's own more abstract description of the music.

To propose the removal of the romantic identification tag might therefore seem unnecessarily puritanical. Yet the name applies purely to the opening movement, with its mysterious arpeggios and trancelike chords which together seem deliberately to conceal the fact that the music, misty and almost motionless though it is, is actually constructed in traditional sonata form. Beethoven, as Alfred Brendel has succinctly put it, 'builds even when he dreams'.

But the dreams did not conceal the truth of the music from the composer. He was clearly aware, as Charles Rosen points out in his book on classical style, that the first movement of the 'Moonlight' was nothing if not extraordinary. Melody and accompaniment are meshed in such a way that it is impossible at times to say which is which. On the one hand, there is the soft – though in piano terms never damped down – triplet figure which is sustained without interruption throughout the movement. On the other, there is the persistent dotted rhythm of what is usually referred to as the 'soprano melody', to which it is umbilically connected.

Then there is the question of how it is all to be pedalled, given that Beethoven's was a very different instrument from the pianos of today. Hector Berlioz, a non-pianist but a composer whose precise sense of instrumental colour has never been surpassed, put it this way: 'The left hand softly displays large chords of a solemn, sad character, and the length of these allows the vibrations of the piano to extend gradually over each one of them.' Since today's pianos differ not only from the ever-changing instruments of Beethoven's day but also from each other, pianists have to work out their own ways of pedalling the music, bearing in mind, as Rosen reminds us, that on modern pianos the pedal cannot be depressed unceasingly in the way Beethoven desired. It is upon such subtle technical details that the magic of a performance depends – and the problem is that no modern pianist, or at any rate no modern piano, can play it delicately enough.

The rest of the work comprises two more movements, each of them requiring a mark-up in tempo. First, leading straight out of the opening adagio, comes a not-so-moonlit, though not unmysterious, interlude which, if played as fast as it often is, sounds like a scherzo. If Beethoven's allegretto marking is respected, however, it is more like a minuet with a curiously offbeat pulse, in which some of the trancelike nature of the opening movement remains. Thereafter, the eruption of the minor-key finale is so sudden and unprecedentedly violent that, if the music can be called nocturnal at all, it is in its evocation of thunder and lightning in a night sky. Nothing like its hammering chords and streaking arpeggios had been written for the piano before. Indeed, Beethoven seems to have composed this music – which, like the first movement, is in disguised sonata form – so impetuously that the very notes in his original manuscript look windswept.

Here, at least, is music the modern concert grand can conspicuously enhance, though you cannot help wondering how many fragile pianos Beethoven himself must have wrecked when trying to achieve the torrents of tone he desired. For all its enduring popularity, however, the work's peculiar poetry remains elusive, and not even the greatest Beethoven interpreters invariably hold the key to it. Alfred Brendel, for instance, can seem so deliberately bold and matter-of-fact in his treatment of the first movement that he walks right past the music's veil of mystery in the recording that forms part of his otherwise exemplary ten-disc boxed set of the sonatas issued in the 1990s (Philips 446 909-2).

Yet the veil of mystery, which is exactly what the great Wilhelm Kempff achieved in the first movement of the 'Moonlight' in his eight-disc box dating from the 1950s, may end up making you long for Brendel's structural and harmonic clarity (DG 447 966-2). My own preference lies with Brendel, not least for the whimsical swing he brings to the second move-ment and the way he rides the storm of the finale. Yet each of these *intégrales*, as the French would call them, of the sonatas is an enthralling journey through one of the greatest of all musical territories, Brendel having the advantage of vivid modern recording and a constantly exhilarating, vividly orchestral approach to the music.

Whether Artur Pizarro, once his set of the sonatas is complete, will join the elite remains to be seen. But the performance of the 'Moonlight' on his first disc shows this Portuguese pianist, winner in 1990 of the Leeds piano competition, to be a single-minded Beethovenian who knows how to pedal as well as play the notes with a virtuosity which never degenerates into selfish ostentation. Although, in partnering the 'Moonlight' with the 'Pathétique', 'Tempest' and 'Appassionata' sonatas, he has stuck to well-trodden paths, the results justify his decision. While he has still to reach his proving ground, these are performances as daring as you could hope for, recorded by a new Scottish company which specialises in high-quality record equipment (Linn Records CKD 209).

Four

1802
SYMPHONY NO. 2 IN D MAJOR, OP. 36

Adagio molto – Allegro con brio   Larghetto

Scherzo: Allegro   Allegro molto

'Artists are fiery by nature and do not weep', declared Beethoven around the time he composed the second of his nine symphonies. And there is much fire, and little weeping, in this remarkable work, which shows no dwindling of inspiration, no loss of nerve, after the impact made by its predecessor, the Symphony No. 1 in C major. Indeed, as the voice of a new century, it speaks far more potently than that infinitely less daring work. For all the lyrical, pastoral sweetness of its slow movement, the Second Symphony contains music quite startlingly progressive and idiosyncratic, often volcanic in energy and humour, a true prelude to the 'Eroica' and an absolutely assured, brilliantly devised masterpiece in its own right.

Yet the yes-declaiming quality of the music, every note of which expresses the power of positive thinking, was quite at odds with the state of Beethoven's mind at the time he wrote it. The quotation at the start of the previous paragraph was no idle statement but part of what has come to be known as Beethoven's 'Heiligenstadt Testament', the famous and harrowing letter in which, from outside Vienna at the age of 32, he admitted that he was going deaf. The music, despite its robustness of outlook, thus dates from one of the most troubled periods in a troubled life, when the composer confessed himself to be contemplating suicide but produced this gloriously sunny and unbuttoned work instead.

Though often described as 'early' Beethoven, and descended though it is from Haydn and Mozart, the Second Symphony needs to be heard in the context of his own music. Like the Third Piano Concerto and 'Moonlight' sonata, which date from the same period, it displays the hand of a vanguard composer for whom the eighteenth century was a thing of the past. The scale of the writing, conspicuously bigger than that of the First Symphony, shows how aware the young Beethoven already was that symphonic form was capable of unprecedented expansion.

Yet there is also a terseness, particularly in the third movement, of a sort to which Beethoven was to return in some of his last string quartets and piano sonatas. The whole work, indeed, is dynamically forward-looking, even if it is content to employ the classical-sized orchestra of the First Symphony, and to make use of recognisably traditional structures –

through which, however, thunderbolts are hurled. Again and again, Beethoven here used conventional procedures in a quite novel way. Each fragment of the scherzo, for instance, is projected by different instruments in a manner prophetic of something for which Schoenberg a century later devised a name – he called it *Klangfarbenmelodie*, meaning a melody dependent more on changes of timbre than on pitch – and which Beethoven coloured, as Berlioz acutely observed, 'with a thousand different tints'.

But the work's originality of utterance is heard in its very opening notes, an orchestral call to attention initially suggestive of Haydn, though soon to prove grander and more emotional as it proceeds towards the rock-face of a hammered-out D minor arpeggio which anticipates the opening of the Ninth Symphony. Trills and triplets sustain the tension until, without a pause, the violins plunge into the seething energy of the main *allegro con brio* portion of the movement. The first subject would sound Mozartian were it not so explosive; the second subject is a quick march in Beethoven's most pungently militaristic vein. The grand, sonorous swell of the coda, with its fierce *fortissimi* and emphatic offbeat chords, shows Beethoven pushing symphonic music into a new age.

To have attended the famous Beethoven benefit concert at the Theater an der Wien in 1803, when this work had its first performance alongside that of the oratorio, *Christ on the Mount of Olives*, and the Third Piano Concerto, with the composer himself as soloist, would have been exhilarating, however scrappy it must have sounded. The First Symphony was also played, and Ferdinand Ries, Beethoven's pupil and early biographer, has left details of a day that started when he was summoned to Beethoven's residence at 5am to find the composer in bed busy revising the orchestration. The rehearsal began three hours later. By 2:20pm, everyone had become cross and impatient; but Prince Lichnowsky, the composer's benefactor, sent for hampers of bread and butter, cold meat and wine. Then the rehearsal resumed, and the concert began at 6pm.

The slow movement, to its first hearers, must have seemed dumbfoundingly large in scale. Edinburgh's distinguished musical essayist, Sir Donald Tovey, has called it 'one of the most luxurious slow movements in the world' – and, if it sometimes sounds Schubertian, that is because Schubert studied it when he came to write his Grand Duo for Piano duet twenty years later. The music progresses unhurriedly, in sonata form, through a lavish succession of themes and repetitions; but the slow, flowing, clarinet-soaked momentum never falters, and makes the scherzo, when finally unleashed, sound all the more concise. This, too, is a movement that later composers plundered (notably Brahms in his D major Serenade).

The rondo finale – with a main theme that crackles like a jumping-jack beneath your feet – manages to cap everything that has gone before. Sir George Grove, in his study of Beethoven's symphonies, exclaimed accurately that No. 2 was 'not so *safe* as No. 1'. As the finale careers to its close, via an array of teasing false endings, you can see just what he meant.

Choosing a recording of the Second Symphony necessitates first deciding whether to buy a boxed set of all nine works, which often carries a considerable price reduction but means you will be stuck with one single conductor who may not be at his best (or to your taste) in every work. If you are prepared to take this risk, you must then decide on whether to choose a traditionally plush performance by a great orchestra and conductor, or something authentically smaller-scale, employing period instruments or at least an element of period style.

The plushest of plush sets has long been Herbert von Karajan's with the Berlin Philharmonic, available on five medium-price discs (DG 429 036-2). Dating from the early 1960s, these are performances which have lost much of their allure, the streamlined style being now as dead as the conductor himself. For a big, sonorously traditional Germanic approach, Gunter Wand and the North German Radio Symphony Orchestra are a better bet. Also on five medium-price discs, these performances are genuinely alive, even if this conductor (until recently a pillar of the Edinburgh Festival) too is dead (RCA 7432189109-5LD).

Closer than either of these conductors to the inner workings of the music, however, is Nikolaus Harnoncourt, through whose keenly detailed performances with the Chamber Orchestra of Europe we are taken to the heart of Beethoven's Vienna. In making these recordings, Harnoncourt has declared, his aim was to waken people up – and the result is the embodiment of Beethoven's fierce, raw, implacable genius. Again, these are on five bargain-price discs, of which in this case you are unlikely to tire (Teldec 2292-46452-2).

Of similar freshness, and likewise to be recommended, are three other complete sets: David Zinman's with the Zurich Tonhalle Orchestra, an improbable rival to the Berlin Philharmonic but here much to be preferred, not least for its use of the often startling new edition of the scores and Beethoven's own controversial metronome markings (Arte Nova 74321 65410-2); Sir John Eliot Gardiner's exhilaratingly hell-for-leather attack on the music with his Orchestre Révolutionnaire et Romantique (DG Archiv 439 900-2); and Sir Charles Mackerras's incisive, alert, thoroughly perceptive performances with the Royal Liverpool Philharmonic (EMI Classics for Pleasure CDBOXLVB 1). All these are five-disc sets, Zinman's being a super-bargain.

These are recordings which are to this writer's taste, and which surely sweep aside most of the starry old names among Beethoven conductors. For a further sample of the modern school of Beethoven conducting, Sir Roger Norrington's treatment of the Second Symphony with the London Classical Players, available as a bargain-price single disc along with a pungent account of the Symphony No. 8 and the *Coriolanus* and *Egmont* overtures, is strongly recommended (Virgin Veritas VM5 61375-2).

Five

1804
SYMPHONY NO. 3 IN E FLAT MAJOR, OP. 55 ('EROICA')

Allegro con brio

Scherzo: Allegro vivace

Marcia funebre: Adagio assai

Finale: Allegro molto

It was inevitable that Beethoven's 'Bonaparte' symphony, as he originally called it, would gather myths. The truth, equally inevitably, is less romantic than the tale of the disillusioned composer slashing the dedicatee's name from the title page when he heard that Napoleon had proclaimed himself emperor. In fact, Beethoven knew the truth about Napoleon two years before he did the erasing, and he restored the name in pencil very soon afterwards. Not until the work was published, a year after the premiere, was the title 'Eroica' added. Had it all, therefore, been just a gesture?

The answer is both yes and no. That Beethoven's views on Napoleon were mixed is not in doubt. That he saw himself as the enlightened musical spokesman for a new century is also clear. His adoption of the Heroic Style in the works of his so-called middle period was evidence of this. But in some respects he was a composer like any other, which meant that he wanted to advance his career to his own benefit, not least because he was going deaf and knew that his days as a great public pianist were numbered.

To suggest that Beethoven, for all his lofty idealism, had basic commercial instincts is not to demean him. He had moved from Bonn to the big musical pond of Vienna, where Mozart had lived on his wits as the world's first great freelance composer. Beethoven's lifestyle was less extravagant than Mozart's, and he notoriously lived in squalor, battling with his landlords in one rented apartment after another. But he was not as poor as he looked. Indeed, he prospered on commissions, on sales of his music, on public concerts and on the support of Viennese aristocrats who wanted to be associated with him. Though the brusque Beethoven's opinions on patronage were well known, he was by no means averse to accepting large dollops of it. He knew that, after a decade in Vienna, he was in demand, and he knew how to use this to his advantage.

But he also knew that Paris was beckoning him. Indeed, the 'Bonaparte' symphony's hidden agendum was that – along with the 'Kreutzer' sonata, intended for the French violinist Rodolphe Kreutzer – its success would ensure him lucrative employment in the French capital, a city he preferred, or thought he did, to Vienna. But it never happened. For some reason, Beethoven went off the idea, and when that happened the symphony's name was changed to the less specific 'Eroica', or 'Heroic', symphony. It seemed, in the circumstances, more an act of self-denial than an expression of contempt for Napoleon. Once he had done it, the die was cast. Vienna would remain his home for the rest of his life. That being so, it would have been politically dangerous for him to show any form of support for a country as threatening as France.

As Maynard Solomon, most perceptive of the composer's modern biographers, has shrewdly put it, 'Beethoven's passport to Viennese citizenship was the rending of the Bonaparte inscription and the consequent merging of his heroic ideal with the national outlook of the Viennese populace'. For Solomon, the deletion of the name, far from being an expression of outrage, was representative of 'a component of caution, an excess of discretion, even a failure of nerve'. Whatever the truth, Beethoven would soon complete his *volte-face* by becoming an outspoken opponent of France.

Yet his private conflict was not over. When Napoleon's brother, who had been appointed king of Westphalia, offered Beethoven the lucrative post of *Kapellmeister*, the composer wavered again. Only the promise of Viennese financial support for life appears to have stopped him accepting.

So how heroic is the 'Eroica'? Or, for that matter, how Napoleonic is it? Not until a year after it was completed in 1805 did the work receive its first performance in Vienna's Theater an der Wien, the setting for several Beethoven premieres. Beethoven was by then 35 years old, and his symphony was the biggest ever written up to that time, with a first movement as long as an entire work by one of his predecessors. That it was no ordinary symphony was clear from the start. Nor was the heroic vigour of the opening movement, reaching a climax of dissonant, disruptive violence in the central development section, in any way in doubt. The sheer scale of this innovatory movement, with its unstoppable momentum and unprecedentedly extended coda, was heroic.

But for whom was the funeral march intended? The music, complete with sonorous oration, is hugely atmospheric and at times thunderously graphic. Napoleon was very much alive when it was written, though Beethoven may have been making the point that all heroes die in the end. He had already composed one heroic but generalised funeral march as the slow movement of his Piano Sonata, Op. 27, No. 1, written in the 'Eroica' key of E flat major – and here was its even grander descendant. After this substantial diversion, the quicksilver scherzo, complete with its whirling trio section for three horns and its slashing cross-rhythms during the scherzo's repeat, retrieves something of the ferocious exuberance of the opening movement.

Dramatic tension is sustained in the finale, traditionally the lightest movement of a symphony, but not on this occasion. The spitfire opening outburst leads to the bare bones of a theme which, when fleshed out, becomes identifiable as one which Beethoven had previously employed in several works. Particularly apposite among these had been his *Prometheus* ballet, whose subject was the civilising ability of art to uplift mankind. Here, then, was the final universal theme of the 'Eroica', delivered as a set of variations filled with vitality, pungent humour and final grandeur. The closing burst of energy rams home its message, which says as much about Beethoven himself, his attitude to the Enlightenment and his ability to live with his deafness as about Napoleon and heroism in general.

Yet it is the heroic side of the 'Eroica' which conductors today find difficult to deal with. It was not a problem for showmen like Herbert von Karajan or Leonard Bernstein, who presented the music in terms of their own vanity. Nor did it bother Karl Boehm, who saw it as part of Austria's glorious musical past, or Wilhelm Furtwangler, for whom, like the Ninth Symphony, it was some sort of mystical rite of passage. Whenever Furtwangler got his fluttering hands on the 'Eroica', flexibility of tempo formed the road to the work's – or his own – inner philosophy.

Among modern conductors, only Daniel Barenboim has followed Furtwangler's path. To others, the heroic aspects of Beethoven can seem an embarrassing irrelevance. Sir Roger Norrington, in his complete recording of the symphonies with the London Classical Players, zooms right past the work in a performance which concentrates on speed and lightness at the expense of significant gestures. It is thoroughly refreshing, though not, in the end, quite interesting enough to seem worth revisiting.

Sir John Eliot Gardiner and the Orchestre Révolutionnaire et Romantique bring a similar breathlessness to their performance, though the similarly speedy David Zinman, with the Zurich Tonhalle Orchestra, supplies keener detail and more surprises. Presenting the first movement in a single sweep may be par for the course nowadays, but his up-tempo funeral march, with its thudding drums, really does sound revolutionary, and his finale has an impish glee which effectively punctures the leanings towards pomposity imposed on the music by other conductors. Coupled with the exuberant and underplayed Symphony No. 4, this is a greatly desirable bargain-price disc (Arte Nova 74321 59214 2). For up-to-the-minute scholarship and style, it is rivalled only by Nikolaus Harnoncourt's similarly illuminating, equally subversive, vividly articulated performance with the Chamber Orchestra of Europe, marred only by a debilitating loss of momentum in the scherzo's trio section (Teldec 3984-28144-2).

Six

1806
PIANO SONATA IN F MINOR, OP. 57 ('APPASSIONATA')

Allegro assai   Andante con moto –   Allegro, ma non troppo – Presto

Like the *Waldstein* sonata, the 'Appassionata' has been called one of the works that brought Beethoven's middle period to the boil. It has also been called the most concise, the most spaciously grand, the most romantic, the most assertively rhetorical, the most tragic and, very interestingly by the pianist Charles Rosen, a sonata whose opening movement is almost rigidly symmetrical in structure, in spite of its violence. It is certainly a milestone in Beethoven's sonata output, and understandably one of the most famous of all his works. Its emphatic air of finality – ten years would pass before he reached the next and very different milestone among his piano sonatas – suggests Beethoven's own recognition that it marked the end of a line.

NOTES ON BEETHOVEN

Though the division of Beethoven's output into three periods — early, middle and late — is now rightly challenged, there is no doubt that the gulf separating the drama of the 'Appassionata' sonata, Op. 57, from the restraint of the A major Sonata, Op. 101, and some of the intervening works, incorporated vast stylistic changes. The danger lies in assuming that late automatically means better, rather than merely different. In fact, the only way to appreciate either of these works is on its own terms, and to accept that they lie on opposite sides of a complicated dividing line. The evocative title of the 'Appassionata', we should remember, was not Beethoven's own, but it is undoubtedly apt and a lot nearer the truth than Tovey's description of the music as 'tragic through and through'. The closest the 'Appassionata' gets to tragedy is not its minor-key ending, which was something that mattered to Tovey, but simply its *King Lear*-like storminess, which is not quite close enough to matter.

Yet it is a tremendous work to have erupted between the calm of the Triple Concerto, Op. 56, and the warmth of the Fourth Piano Concerto, Op. 58. Even the report by Beethoven's pupil Ferdinand Ries of how the composer 'hummed and howled' the torrential semiquavers of the finale during a walk together, and how, on returning home, he rushed to the piano to pound out the notes on the keyboard without taking off his hat, suggests that they must have struck him like lightning.

But the knowledge that he was simultaneously sketching the imprisoned Florestan's dungeon scene in *Fidelio* suggests something else, at least about the first movement's opening descent to the lowest note on the keyboard (the finale of Op. 101 goes a semitone lower, thanks to the superior keyboard by then available). The hollowness of this opening motif results from the notes being played two octaves apart – a striking effect. The second subject, when it arrives, sounds like a heroic major-key inversion of the first. The fact that it appears to have been an inspired afterthought stresses again the powerful improvisational nature of the music. Or does it? The observant Charles Rosen, after all, considers the first movement to be so scrupulously assembled that it falls into four unmistakably clear-cut sections – exposition, development, recapitulation, coda – each of them beginning with the main theme.

The central andante, a short set of variations, is not so much a slow movement as an introduction to the finale, though its steady progress towards its climax again suggests something very carefully planned. The finale itself proves every bit as turbulent as Ries's description of its genesis makes it seem. Yet, even after it appears to have run its swirling course, it is not quite over. With a grinding change of gear, the speed increases and the music – as the finale of the Seventh Symphony would also do – heads straight for the abyss.

Not all Beethoven pianists find the up-front energy of the 'Appassionata' sonata completely to their taste. Of those who revel in it, some superimpose a glamour on it which is foreign to the spirit of the music. Beethoven was not Liszt, though he was certainly an influence on his leonine successor. In his recent conversation book, *The Veil of Order*, Alfred Brendel calls the 'Appassionata' a 'painterly' work, and it is easy to see what he means. It does not tell a story, it does not directly evoke a picture, but it presents its material with a painterly command of musical image and colour which can only be called magnificent. Placing it among the five Beethoven sonatas which he considers to be 'especially perfect and rounded', Brendel says that no matter how often it is performed, it is a masterpiece 'from which there is no escaping'. Its grip, both for performer and listener, is inexorable.

But it is also – and this, too, is a factor Brendel puts his finger on precisely – a work in which what is expressed is 'indissolubly linked' to the technical execution. Everything meshes, which is what makes Brendel's own performances of it sound so firmly focused, so finely balanced, strong but unflashy. Amid the cluster of popular sonatas included in a two-disc bargain-price recording from the 1970s, its execution is as arresting as its subject matter. It is not virtuosity for its own sake, but piano technique which illuminates everything to which it is applied. With the 'Pathétique', 'Moonlight', 'Tempest', 'Pastoral' and 'Les Adieux' as companion pieces, this is a greatly desirable survey of Beethoven's road towards his middle period and road out of it again, with the 'Appassionata' the major point of focus (Philips 438 730-2).

Few of Brendel's juniors, though an ample number of his defunct seniors, reveal such grasp of the 'Appassionata'. The start of a new cycle from Artur Pizarro, who is devoting a year of his life to the performance of the thirty-two works, bodes well, however. The four works, including the 'Appassionata', on his first disc are linked by the fact that all are in minor keys and are sonatas with familiar nicknames. But, far from making them seem assembly-line offerings, the former Leeds prizewinner brings to them the most meticulous attention and sharpness of response (Linn Records CKD 209).

NOTES ON BEETHOVEN

We all have our mental pictures of Beethoven the pianist, based partly on the comments of his contemporaries, partly on the sort of piano music he wrote. Yet inevitably these pictures are contradictory. The sparkle of his C major Piano Concerto, after all, is different from the drama of his C minor. The intimacy of the G major is different from the heroism of what we in Britain like to call the 'Emperor' concerto. How do we identify these four sorts of Beethoven – five if we include the further contradictions of the early B flat major Concerto – with the man whom Weber saw as a deaf, scowling recluse, surrounded by squalor and battering at his piano so as to force the sound of it through to his brain?

That was Beethoven at the age of 53, by which time the composing of concertos was a thing of the past and he had progressed to the world of the Missa Solemnis and the last string quartets. Yet, even in his youth, Beethoven's playing had been described by his friend Franz Wegeler as 'rude and hard', though others heard him differently. Willibrord Mahler, the portrait painter, spoke of how he played with his hands very still: 'wonderful though his execution was, there was no tossing of them to and fro, up and down; they seemed to glide right and left, over the keys, the fingers alone doing the work'. In 1795, at the age of 25, Beethoven made his first major concert appearance in Vienna, playing – indeed to some extent improvising – his own B flat major Piano Concerto. He had arrived there two years earlier, as a novice from Bonn, and had already drawn attention to himself in the salons of the city. As a pianist, composer and improviser, he was considered someone worth watching. His performance of the B flat Concerto – which, though published as his second work in the form, was in fact his first – confirmed expectations. He seemed destined to become the finest pianist in Europe, though not necessarily the finest composer.

By 1802, however, his destiny had changed. He had discovered that he was going deaf. But, as his career as a great public performer diminished, so his career as a great composer expanded. To what extent he would have been a different composer had he not gone deaf, we shall never know. The heroic style he cultivated in the first years of the nineteenth century, in such works as the 'Eroica' symphony and the 'Waldstein' sonata, the latter written in response to improvements in the size and quality of Viennese pianos, reflected both his revolutionary tendencies as a composer and his battle with his encroaching deafness.

Seven

1806
PIANO CONCERTO NO. 4 IN G MAJOR, OP. 58

Allegro moderato   Andante con moto –   Rondo: Vivace

Beethoven, it is safe to say, did not perform his Fourth Piano Concerto quite so 'poetically' as most soloists perform it today. True, the special circumstances of its first public performance on 22 December 1808 may have acted against a lyrical, unhurried approach to the music, such as we are now accustomed to. Coming at the end of the concert's very long first half – and in an unheated Theater an der Wien which was growing colder by the minute – it was unlikely to make the composer feel inclined to linger over the work's fine detail, especially as the premiere of the Fifth Symphony, followed by that of the 'Pastoral', lay immediately ahead.

As Joseph Reichardt – the Berlin composer, author and acutely observant member of the first-night audience – was later to write, Beethoven performed the concerto 'astonishingly well at the fastest possible tempos', even though the solo part was clearly of 'monstrous difficulty'. No doubt the quantity of embellishments Beethoven added for the occasion contributed to the impression of complexity, prompting the composer Karl Czerny, who was also present, to describe Beethoven's playing as 'roguish' – hardly a word which a commentator would be likely to apply to a performance of this concerto today, but again carrying an implication of speed rather than meditation.

Yet the intensity of Beethoven's playing could not have been generated merely by the work's newness. In fact, it was not quite new, having been written two years previously and having already been privately performed. But, in the short space of time between his third and fourth piano concertos, he had been frenetically busy, producing the 'Eroica' symphony, the 'Waldstein', 'Appassionata' and 'Kreutzer' sonatas, and the three 'Razumovsky' quartets. In addition, he had been frustratedly beating *Fidelio* into shape and wrestling with his increasing deafness. Whatever the meaning of the fourth concerto's curiously pictorial slow movement – Orpheus taming the Furies has always been thought to be its secret message – its juxtaposition of impatience and patience could symbolise Beethoven's own life at the time.

But the entire work is really a study in opposites, the gently oblique opening of the first movement transforming itself, at the start of the recapitulation, into a grand, triumphant and by no means oblique statement of the same material. The finale likewise is serene and vivacious on the one hand, loud and bludgeoning on the other. Too many commentators, in calling this the most 'feminine' of Beethoven's piano concertos, ignore its macho side, which Toscanini knew how to emphasise when he conducted it.

Yet the poetry of the opening bars is not to be gainsaid, even if the rhythm of the main theme – though not its mood – is almost identical to the opening of the Fifth Symphony. The one work, indeed, is in some ways the obverse of the other, as the audience in 1808 was bound to notice. Though the Fifth Symphony famously startled its first listeners, the concerto also has its vanguard features, albeit of a less sensational nature.

Never before had a composer begun a concerto with a piano solo, and a barely audible one at that. The orchestra's entry in an audibly alien key is no less surprising. Within a few quiet bars, then, Beethoven destroyed all his audience's preconceptions about concerto form. The first movement's ceaselessly modulating exposition similarly keeps its listeners guessing. The piano's recently extended keyboard is gloriously exploited in music filled with ethereal sweetness, though the material is also energised by much use of sparkling triplet figures.

The short andante, an enigmatic dialogue between piano and strings, may represent no more than a soft answer turning away wrath. The strings start with a scowl, or at least with the starkness of some of Vivaldi's slow movements, and the piano responds with balm. But gradually the strings relent and the piano, with a final eloquent plea, wins the debate. Then, via one of Beethoven's seemingly perverse modulations, from E minor to C major in the context of a G major concerto, the finale begins without a break. In structure, it is one of Beethoven's characteristically idiosyncratic rondos. The main theme starts in one key and ends in another. The humour is sometimes pungent, sometimes mellow, the final surge of energy sunlit and exhilarating. Yet there is an irascible quality which lies just below the surface of this music, ever ready to erupt and to remind you who the composer is.

In no other Beethoven concerto is subtle integration between soloist and orchestra more crucial than here. The right conductor for the music is therefore as important as the right soloist. A star pianist, performing egotistically to the strains of what is no more than an orchestral 'accompaniment', gives no more than an impression of what this concerto is about.

Nikolaus Harnoncourt, in his recording with Pierre-Laurent Aimard as soloist issued in 2003, is one of the few conductors – just as Aimard is one of the few pianists – who positively make this point. Based on a concert performance given in the Austrian city of Graz with the young Chamber Orchestra of Europe, the result is a miracle of subtle cohesion. Aimard, who specialises in the music of Messiaen and Ligeti, may seem an unexpected choice for a Beethoven concerto, but it pays off in the high clarity of his playing and the way it is balanced with an orchestra significantly smaller than tradition dictates.

Yet nothing sounds weak, no detail is obscured, no texture left unexplored, no point missed. The performance is never in danger of losing itself in self-contemplation – and when it erupts, which is quite often, it erupts powerfully. By scrupulous control of tempo, both pianist and conductor conspire to obtain playing which is both energetic and lyrical, with splendidly punchy *fortissimi*, perfectly graded *pianissimi* and the most startling attention to pauses. Harnoncourt's timing of each separate strand of the slow movement contributes as much as anything else to the starkness of its success and makes you realise how sloppily it is usually treated. This is Beethoven playing of the utmost freshness, in which innumerable points of detail are clarified to the benefit of the work as a whole. For those who do not already know this concerto, here is a wonderful way to learn it. For those who know and love it, it is a revelation.

The performance comes as part of a three-disc box, along with Beethoven's four other piano concertos. With its combination of Austrian authority and French illumination, this medium-price set is definitely the one to buy (Teldec 0927 47334-2). But there are also single discs worth hearing. Murray Perahia, partnered by Bernard Haitink and the Amsterdam Concertgebouw Orchestra, is a pristine soloist in a recording which finds space for the more extrovert 'Emperor' concerto as coupling (Sony SMK 89711). Equally rewarding is Alfred Brendel's genuine musical dialogue –

strong, serious, lucidly articulated — with Sir Simon Rattle and the Vienna Philharmonic, this time with a gripping account of the early C major Piano Concerto as coupling (Philips 462 782-2).

Eight

1806
STRING QUARTET IN F MAJOR, OP. 59,
No. 1 ('RAZUMOVSKY')

Allegro

Adagio molto e mesto –

Allegretto vivace e sempre scherzando

Allegro

Beethoven's three 'Razumovsky' quartets belong to what is traditionally called his 'middle period', along with the subsequent E flat major quartet, Op. 74, nicknamed the 'Harp', and the F minor, Op. 95, which Beethoven himself called his *Quartetto serioso*. But 'middle period', when applied to Beethoven and similarly to Verdi, has always been a loose description, which today seems even looser. It fits the 'Razumovsky' quartets to perfection, however, in that it underlines the startling difference between them and the six shorter Opus 18 quartets, completed only five years earlier in 1801. Though these in themselves had seemed startling enough portents of a new century, his style had continued to develop. By the time he reached his 'Razumovsky' quartets, he had changed the face of European music for ever. But by the time he reached Opus 95, theoretically a middle-period work, he was changing it again.

The switch from Beethoven's first to second period (to employ a different description) had been represented by his growing individuality in its more extreme and affirmative manifestations. This was obviously more conspicuous in the big orchestral sonorities of the 'Eroica' symphony and the attention-seeking clamour of the 'Waldstein' piano sonata, but it was present in the 'Razumovsky' quartets, too. By the time he wrote them, he was 36 years old – already older than Mozart was when he died – and in the process of reconciling himself to the deafness that had struck him some years earlier. 'Let your deafness no longer remain a secret, even in art', he jotted on one of his sketches for these works.

Beethoven composed his Opus 59 triptych for a Russian aristocrat, Count Andreas Kyrilovich Razumovsky, and in tribute to their dedicatee he made subtle use in them of some Russian themes. Yet in character the three works are contrasted rather than unified. The first, in F major, is broad and singing, the second in E minor plaintive and passionate, the third in C major brilliant and athletic. Together they could be said to form a kind of Beethovenian answer to Mozart's last three symphonies, equally clearly composed as a group. Though hailed by the Leipzig *Allgemeine Musikalische Zeitung*, the most important music magazine of the period, as 'profoundly thought through and admirably worked out', their boldness of style did not win immediate widespread approval. One cellist, when faced with the scherzo of the F major quartet, threw his music on the floor and stamped on it with rage. Indeed, so many people considered these works to be the ravings of a madman that Beethoven felt obliged to declaim his famous words: 'Not for you, but for a later age.'

Listening to the serene, poised, long-spun melody with which the cello sets the first movement of the F major quartet in motion, we may wonder what all the fuss was about. Yet the vast scale of this work, and its expansion of quartet technique through its virtuoso use of all four instruments, daunted many of its early performers and listeners. Melodically it is rich and beautiful, but the unfolding of its argument is leisurely at times almost to the point of what must have seemed like disintegration. Of all Beethoven's great quartets, it is the one that still places the greatest physical demands on its performers – more even than the big introvert works of his last years. Interviewed by the writer of this book, the leader of the Amadeus Quartet once admitted that this work and Schubert's similarly exhausting G major Quartet were two pieces he and his colleagues endeavoured never to take on tour.

For listeners, at least, its rewards are now less stressful. The entire opening allegro seems to grow from the cello melody with which it begins, though an important role is also given to a series of mysterious chords, moving softly from one register to another. The movement – like, surprisingly, each succeeding movement of this quartet – possesses a classical sonata-form structure, and towards its close there is a climactic, grandly exhilarating and sustained statement of the main theme, *fortissimo* on all four instruments.

The second movement is a species of scherzo, making witty use of a little rhythmic pattern first heard, in soft staccato notes, on the cello. Most of the music is concerned with this and similar patterns, with the emphasis sometimes on melody, sometimes on bare rhythm, sometimes on quick changes of key. In places, the persistently detached, staccato sound gives way to something smoother and more sustained; and there are moments when the soft whirring of the instruments erupts into brief, characteristically pungent outbursts.

In the slow movement, the key changes to F minor for a long lament, somewhat reminiscent of the 'Eroica' symphony's funeral march. On his sketches for this adagio, Beethoven wrote: 'A weeping willow or acacia over the grave of my brother'; but the precise significance of the statement is a little obscure, since two of his brothers were still alive, and the third had died long ago in infancy. Some authorities claim that the music is an 'epitaph' on Carl van Beethoven's marriage, because Beethoven grumpily detested his brother's bride; others prefer to believe that he was actually remembering his baby brother Georg, who had died in Bonn. At any rate, the movement is grave, sombre and touching – a long sad song, throbbingly sung, with radical use of pizzicato notes expressly for emotional effect.

Towards the end of the adagio, the first violin breaks away from the rest of the ensemble with an airy, ornate cadenza that lightens the mood, brings the key back to F major and ushers in the finale, a vivacious allegro inspired principally by the 'Russian theme' (thus marked in the score) with which it begins. This polka-like melody, first played somewhat tentatively by the cello beneath a series of trills on the first violin, is put dashingly, not to say swashbucklingly, through its paces. Then, just before the end, the speed slackens and the violin, at the top of its register, sings it nostalgically, for the last time, at the sort of speed a Russian folk singer might consider appropriate. Depending on how the players treat it, it is a beautiful effect and a reminder that, from the very beginning, singing lines have been a vital feature of this long quartet.

Beethoven's middle quartets, by their very nature, have qualities not only of progress but of consolidation about them. Intense, idiomatic, original, they are the work of a composer who has found his style and developed it to a high level of technical assurance and emotional expression. Drawn-out string chords, leaping melodies, violent rhythms, rapt slow movements conceived to perfection in quartet terms – these are among the features of the music which players have to contend with, recognising that the works originally demanded something new and special. They are not the same as the Opus 18 quartets, nor are they the same as the late works. To call them more extrovert would be tempting, yet in their slow movements they are not extrovert at all.

The Emerson Quartet, in its recording of Op. 59, No. 1, is fast and forthright, emotionally supercharged, every rhythm and accent articulated to the highest effect. This is modern American playing – what one critic has called the Manhattan style – at its most brilliant. To achieve maximum concentration and power, all but the cellist play standing up, and the first and second violinists alternate as leaders of the ensemble. The effect is magnificently alive, but sometimes it makes you feel you have been run over by a train. With this proviso, the three-disc set of the middle quartets can be enthusiastically recommended, not least for the jet-propelled account of the finale of the third 'Razumovsky', an unmatchable tour de force (DG 453 764-2).

Yet Hungary's fine young Takács Quartet in a rival recording, also on three discs, achieves as much without sounding quite so glossy or overheated (Decca 470 847-2); and there is a glorious intimacy in the performances by the Juilliard Quartet (three-disc set of the middle-period works, Sony SB3K89896). Both these sets give the impression that they are being played, with deep concentration, to a handful of listeners in a room rather than a concert hall.

Nine

1806
VIOLIN CONCERTO IN D MAJOR, OP. 61

Allegro ma non troppo   Larghetto –   Rondo: Allegro

The piano was Beethoven's instrument, the one upon which he proved himself to be the most startling young soloist and improviser of the day, and for which he composed the bulk of his sonatas, concertos and sets of variations. But, like Haydn and Mozart before him, he had also studied the violin, played in an orchestra in his native Bonn, and learned enough about it to produce, in Vienna in 1806, what posterity has decreed to be the greatest of all violin concertos.

Nowhere near adroit enough to perform the work himself, he entrusted its premiere to Franz Clement, leader of the orchestra at the famous Theater an der Wien, where it was baptised two days before Christmas, with Beethoven as conductor. Clement, it is traditionally claimed, was a raffish figure, given to feats of showmanship such as improvising a sonata or set of variations on one string with his violin turned upside down.

Doubtless it was the latter trick of the trade which prompted Beethoven to inscribe on the manuscript of his concerto the pun: 'Concerto per Clemenza pour Clement.' Happily, Clement gave Beethoven the clemency he sought. The story that he inserted one of his own freakish works between the first movement and slow movement of the new concerto belongs to the realms of Beethoven mythology. Clement did have his moment of wizardry, but not until later in the substantial programme, where it could do no harm.

Nor could he be blamed for any shortcomings in the performance of the concerto itself. He was, by all accounts, a violinist of exceptional finesse and lightness of touch, the possessor of an uncannily accurate memory (after a few performances of Haydn's *Creation*, he wrote down the entire score, making the composer fear that he had access to a pirated edition), and was thoroughly versed in Beethoven's music. Having conducted the premiere of the 'Eroica' symphony the previous year and been leader of the orchestra at the premiere of *Fidelio*, he was undaunted by the fact that the score of the concerto was finished only a day or two before he played it. If the concerto did not fully establish itself until Joseph Joachim performed it in London almost forty years later with Mendelssohn as conductor, the reason surely lay in its great length and high originality.

Beethoven's may have been a pianist's violin concerto – so were Brahms's and Mendelssohn's – but he wrote it with a deep love for the instrument, creating a serene and perfectly structured masterpiece that bears no hint of the haste in which it was completed. True, it is not quite so serene as it seems. The tendency among certain soloists – the late Yehudi Menuhin springs particularly to mind – to turn the music into a slow, soulful, spiritual experience does Beethoven no favours. In such circumstances, the first movement ends up sounding seriously over-extended, the slow movement beautiful but inert. As the pianist Alfred Brendel has asserted in a different context, there is an element of the circus about all concertos, and this one is no exception. People who grow devotional on listening to it should bear in mind that Clement was its first and chosen exponent.

The work is as precisely focused in its tiny details (such as delaying the use of pizzicato notes until the finale, and then using them in just one single bar) as in its famously long-spun lines. In no way does it sound like a concerto worked out at the keyboard and then adapted for violin. Indeed, you have only to listen to the composer's own subsequent transcription of it for piano and orchestra (which he agreed to prepare for his British publisher, in the belief that a piano version would help to improve its foreign sales) to realise how wrong the music sounds in a medium other than the one for which it was conceived.

Clement clearly had the qualities Beethoven wanted for a concerto such as this. As one commentator has remarked: 'Tone, not display, is its secret.' True, but what sort of tone? The work dates from one of the most assertive and productive periods in his life, the so-called 'middle' period, during which he had already written the first version of *Fidelio*, the 'Eroica' symphony, the Fourth Piano Concerto, the three 'Razumovsky' string quartets, and the thirty-two piano variations in C minor. In mood, it may seem to correspond most closely to the Fourth Piano Concerto, another work less serene than it is traditionally made to sound, while treating its material with a similar spaciousness of design. The soloist's entry in the first movement is delayed until what seems like the last possible moment, and not until the coda is he/she permitted to play the wondrous (and wondrously simple) second theme in its entirety.

The first movement's binding factor is the rhythm of the five soft drum-taps heard at the outset. Tossed from section to section of the orchestra, this motif underpins, punctuates and inspires the wealth of themes from which Beethoven builds the music, adding a high clarity of definition to a movement otherwise dependent, or so it would seem, on lyrical flow.

The larghetto in G major, though only ninety-two bars long, has the sweet stillness found in some of Beethoven's other great slow movements, that of the 'Emperor' concerto springing particularly to mind. But stillness does not necessarily mean slowness, and larghetto, it should be remembered, is faster than adagio. Played at the right speed, its progress (based largely on a series of meditative variations on the muted opening theme) is soon interrupted by bold orchestral chords, dramatically signalling the movement's end and the return of the home key of D major. These lead without a break to the genial finale, a rondo with a rocking main theme in 6/8 time, with contrasted episodes (one of them employing a solo bassoon to droll yet curiously poignant effect) and a radiance of expression that anticipates the finale of the 'Pastoral' symphony, composed two years later.

On disc, there are plenty of slow performances of the Violin Concerto but very few fast ones. Among the former, Itzhak Perlman's with Carlo Maria Giulini and the Philharmonia Orchestra never drags and, recorded in 1980, finds soloist and conductor still at the height of their powers (EMI CDM5 66900-2). Of the fast ones, Jascha Heifetz's with Toscanini and the NBC Symphony Orchestra is certainly the front-runner. Clocking in at under forty minutes, it brings an exhilarating momentum to the first movement which, though recorded in 1940, shows the music in completely fresh light. The recently cleaned-up recording quality makes this disc, which has space for Brahms's Violin Concerto as a filler, a serious, bargain-price contender (Naxos 8 110936).

Thomas Zehetmair, one of today's most fascinating violinists, is also conspicuously zippy in the first movement, with Frans Bruggen and the Orchestra of the Eighteenth Century supplying vivacious support (Philips 462 123-2). For the brightest articulation, most passionate conviction and glorious unpredictability, however, Gidon Kremer is the soloist to go for. In his performance with Nikolaus Harnoncourt and the Chamber Orchestra of Europe, he displays a lightness of touch which inevitably makes you think of him as a reincarnation of Clement, not least when he plays his own violin transcription of the vanguard cadenza, complete with piano and kettledrums, which Beethoven wrote for the piano version of the concerto. To some – perhaps many – ears, this may sound unacceptably bizarre. Yet it is the only available cadenza (Beethoven having failed to supply any other) which could be said to be authentic. The recording (Teldec 3984 28144-2) forms part of Harnoncourt's bargain-price ten-disc collection of Beethoven's nine symphonies and other works.

Ten

1808
SYMPHONY NO. 5 IN C MINOR, OP. 67

Allegro con brio   Andante con moto   Allegro –   Allegro

Leonard Bernstein, in one of his television lectures which were often so much sharper than his performances, had this to say about the first four notes of Beethoven's Fifth Symphony: 'Three Gs and an E flat. Simple. Baby simple. Anybody could think of it. Maybe.'

In these words he underlined the reverberating impact of a motif Beethoven had already employed, to quite different and less sensational effect, in his Fourth Piano Concerto and other works. Beethoven's own comment, as quoted by his unreliable friend Anton Schindler, was that in the Fifth Symphony the notes represented Fate rapping at the door.

The words, true or otherwise, were vivid enough to go down in history, along with the V-for-victory symbolism of the notes in Morse code during the Second World War. Even if the motif was an established Beethoven fingerprint at a certain stage in his career, he never used it more potently than in this symphony, where it obsessively pervades the opening movement and returns, in slightly altered form, in both the scherzo and finale. It was a motif which, in any case, had already been heroically employed by Cherubini in his *Hymne du Panthéon*, as Beethoven, an ardent admirer of that Paris-based Italian, surely knew. The fierce thematic unity of the first movement of the Fifth Symphony is nevertheless its strongest feature, transcending not only Cherubini's but also Beethoven's own previous use of it.

Hurled at us in increasingly pungent C minor, it makes its point unequivocally and goes on making it. Not even the forlorn little oboe cadenza which intrudes at the height of the action can impede its progress for long. When the motif immediately resumes, its fury is doubled. But whether, as has often been claimed, the music's inexorably marching motion represents Austria expelling the French is hard to say. Certainly, although some listeners are unwilling to see it as hawkish, this is a profoundly militaristic and devastating work – and the brassy fanfares in the slow movement, the screaming piccolo and braying trombones in the finale, are in themselves enough to confirm the fact.

Not for nothing did a member of the Napoleonic guard, on hearing it for the first time, reputedly spring misguidedly to his feet at the start of the finale, crying 'C'est l'empereur'. The music is ceremonial, exultant, even brutal, an exercise in triumphalism of the most blatant sort, summed up by the modish saying that if you have a hammer, you find nails to use it on. In this symphony, Beethoven had his hammer. How the music actually sounded as part of an under-rehearsed four-hour Beethoven programme in an unheated Theater an der Wien in December 1808 is anybody's guess. But, however inaccurate the performance, and however uncomfortable the conditions in which it took place, its message must have been clear.

Beethoven, who had once contemplated settling in Paris rather than Vienna, held famously self-contradictory views on Napoleon, as well as possessing a considerable admiration for French music. And it was Berlioz, a Frenchman, who said that Beethoven's ability to sustain such a height of effect in this work was nothing if not 'prodigious'. Yet it took a long time – four years, from 1804 until 1808 – for him to shape the symphony to his satisfaction while distracting himself with other major projects.

During the long gestation of what is by no means a long work, the slow movement, originally conceived as a sort of lumbering minuet, eventually became a theme and variations through whose often brazen notes a hint of dance motion remained discernible. The scherzo, originally an extended movement on the lines of the scherzos of the fourth, sixth and seventh symphonies, eventually grew shorter – though Pierre Boulez and Nikolaus Harnoncourt, in their recordings of it, have continued to champion the full-length version of this movement which, it is now thought, may have been erroneously abbreviated. The finale, linked to the scherzo by ghostly drum-taps, stealthy strings and the gradual appearance of what seems like a pale thread of light, announces itself with the most resounding burst of C major in musical history.

Yet the work as a whole is not purely about progress from the sombreness of C minor to the fierce sunshine of the major key. The four notes with which it opens – those three Gs and an E flat – are not specifically in the key of C minor at all, even if that is how they sound. Nor are they played by the full orchestra, though that is the effect which their initial statement on strings and clarinets manages to convey. There are performances, more often now than in the past, which can make the victory of C major over C minor seem quite irrelevant, the whole work being a show of bombastic force. Beethoven's Fifth may be the most familiar, or over-familiar, of all his symphonies, but a good performance of it still has the power to surprise.

Recordings of the Fifth tend to fall between well-upholstered, romantic, old-fashioned performances about good banishing evil, and harder-edged, smaller-scale modern performances in which the heroic side of Beethoven is taken with a pinch of salt. Though all music is subject to fashion, the latter approach, at least for the moment, seems nearer the truth. Beethoven's Fifth is not a beautiful work but a raw, abrasive one, and the sounds it makes have nothing to do with his diminished hearing. He heard it that way in his head.

Nikolaus Harnoncourt's with the Chamber Orchestra of Europe is a performance for today, guaranteed to chill as much as to exhilarate, and thus a milestone in Beethoven interpretation. The smallness of the orchestra proves in no way incompatible with intensity of expression. Indeed, the reverse is true. The clarity of texture, moreover, is like an X-ray of Beethoven's mind, revealing, among much else, that the solo oboe cadenza in the first movement, far from coming as a surprise, has been plaintively audible inside the music for several bars beforehand. The extended version of the scherzo and the inclusion of the big exposition repeat in the finale (which many conductors continue to consider unnecessary) add to the powerful circling motion of the performance. Whether in the complete set of the symphonies – which is the way to buy it – or on a single disc, this is the performance to have (Teldec 3984-28144-2).

For a more traditional, less disturbing but impressively incisive performance, Carlos Kleiber's bargain-price recording with the Vienna Philharmonic is recommended. It is justly famous and durable (Kleiber, one of the finest but most unwilling conductors in the world, came out of semi-hiding to record it in the 1970s). As a further incentive, a pulverising account of the Seventh Symphony is included as coupling (DG 447 400-2).

Eleven

1808
SYMPHONY NO. 6 IN F MAJOR, OP. 68 ('PASTORAL')

Allegro ma non troppo   Andante molto mosso

Allegro –   Allegro –   Allegretto

There were pastoral symphonies before Beethoven's. Handel's – a single movement for strings – formed a peaceful interlude in Part One of *Messiah*, a work Beethoven loved. Justin Heinrich Knecht's *Musical Portrait of Nature*, written in 1785, possessed descriptive movement headings almost identical to those used by Beethoven twenty-four years later (indeed, it is now accepted that Beethoven spotted Knecht's descriptions in an advertisement on the same page of a journal listing some of Beethoven's own sonatas). Franz Jacob Freystädtler's *Morning*, *Midday and Evening*, written in the year of Mozart's death, contained a *ranz des vaches*, or 'cow-herd's song', on which Beethoven may have modelled the finale of his symphony. Vivaldi's

NOTES ON BEETHOVEN

Four Seasons, fountainhead of many picturesque works of its kind, reveals further similarities.

The point about Beethoven's 'Pastoral', however, is that it is not just nature music or, as the acid Hans Keller said of the four Vivaldi concertos, 'background music with nothing in the foreground'. Berlioz, who claimed to be more profoundly affected by it than by any of Beethoven's other symphonies, called it 'an astounding landscape that seems to have been composed by Poussin and painted by Michelangelo'. Beethoven himself preferred to think of it as 'more an expression of feeling than a painting'. Either way, it is the most tranquil of his symphonies, its famous storm scene being a brief interlude rather than a full-scale symphonic movement.

With its euphonious, often static harmonies, and with little emphasis on violent, hammered-out rhythms, it is also quite deliberately the simplest of all Beethoven's symphonies. Why, then, should it be hailed as a crucial work in his output? Partly because it captures, with glowing eloquence, a side of his musical personality no other work conveys so consummately; partly because it is so lovable; and partly because it is more progressive than it seems. In the central development section of the first movement, where a work such as the 'Eroica' symphony practically tears itself apart, Beethoven does the opposite and lets nothing happen at all. As an anticipation of the modern minimalist school of composition, its pattering repetitions, floating free of tension through different keys, are a stroke of genius.

In a first movement so conspicuously free of clashes between major and minor, the work may seem to confirm the handed-down belief that Beethoven's even-numbered symphonies are less sensational, and therefore less interesting, than the odd-numbered ones. But it all depends on what is meant by sensation. Played with vitality, the even-numbered symphonies can sound very sensational indeed, and the 'Pastoral' has a glowing warmth of utterance which sets it apart from all the others. Yet the simplicity is counterbalanced by the subtle shades of the orchestration. It was not for nothing that Berlioz adored the 'Pastoral' symphony – and many passages of his own *Symphonie Fantastique* (especially in the slow 'Scène aux Champs') reflect his admiration.

Part of it was written simultaneously with the Fifth Symphony, to which it acts as a relaxed and lyrical complement. It was completed in 1808 in what is now the Viennese suburb of Heiligenstadt, where Beethoven had first grappled with deafness, and which was then still 'a charming village, with a view across meadows to the Danube and the far Carpathians'. Its first performance took place in December of that year, in the same four-hour concert in a freezing Theater an der Wien as the premiere of the Fifth Symphony.

The music, again anticipating Berlioz's *Symphonie Fantastique*, is laid out in five movements instead of Beethoven's standard four, though the last three movements are linked to form a single poetic vision of rustic merry-making (scherzo), sudden storm, and hymn of thanksgiving to God after the storm. But the earlier movements, too, show the composer as poetic observer, unhurriedly communing with nature, and (as his notebooks have it) hearing every tree murmur to him 'Holy, holy'.

The first movement, 'Awakening of Happy Feelings on Arriving in the Country', sprouts from the fresh, tripping tune sung by the violins in the opening bars. Berlioz detected here flocks of chattering birds, air laden with vapours, and sunshine flooding the fields and woods with torrents of dazzling splendour. Though we need not read these precise sounds and pictures into the music – which follows, in spite of its placid development section, the standard progress of sonata form – it is easy to share Berlioz's responses.

The slow movement, 'By the Brook', finds Beethoven pausing for lengthy meditation, again in sonata form. The lower strings intone a flowing accompaniment in swaying 12/8 time, maintained for most of the movement and placidly evoking the brook beside which the composer is lingering. Anton Schindler, Beethoven's Boswell, has described what he believed to be the exact spot in the Heiligenstadt valley that was the source of the composer's inspiration: 'A limpid stream descended from a neighbouring height, shaded on both banks by leafy elms.' The main theme floats serenely on the surface of the stream; and, so far as the woodwind are concerned, this is a movement of bird-calls. Indeed, to particularise the point, flute, oboe and clarinet are given a combined cadenza just before the close, where (as Beethoven himself indicated) they depict the song of the nightingale, quail and cuckoo.

The third movement is a scherzo, 'Peasants' Merry-making', in which humanity at last intrudes on the idyllic landscape, and the music becomes increasingly bucolic. The opening dance-tune is worked up to a climax and succeeded by a trio section in which the woodwind emulate an inept village band in which the oboe keeps missing the beat and the bassoon is incapable of uttering more than a basic cadence in the key of F. The time changes briefly to two beats in a bar for a stamping square dance, after which there is a complete reprise of the foregoing material. Even the trio section comes round a second time, in one of Beethoven's circling symphonic double repetitions.

But this is not the third movement's only surprise. Towards the end, the scherzo starts for a third time, but the music suddenly begins to go askew, the speed accelerates and, in a headlong *presto*, we are swept into the storm, whose effect is heightened by the addition of piccolo, trombones and kettledrums. Hushed tremolos and rainy rhythms from the strings disperse the rustic revellers, then for 125 jagged bars the storm blows strongly, with sonorities deliberately sharper than the pastoral tonics and dominants of the rest of the work.

With soothing tones from oboe and strings, the skies finally clear, and a fluttering upward scale from the flute ushers in the finale, 'Shepherd's Song, Happy and Thankful Feelings after the Storm'. Clarinet and horn play a *ranz des vaches* (a melody with which cow-herds call their cattle) and out of this grows a calm rondo theme on the violins. Towards the end, while the lower strings stride upwards through great arpeggios, the music reaches a solemn, shining climax and then subsides into a whispered nocturnal variation of the main theme. A muted horn recalls the *ranz des vaches*, and the symphony is over.

Again, Nikolaus Harnoncourt's recording with the Chamber Orchestra of Europe is nothing short of a revelation in its attention to the music's fine detail, its sweetness of woodwind tone and beauty of phrasing. But it is not a soft sell. The storm blazes fiercely, and there is a rhythmic vitality even in the slow movement which prevents the symphony from sounding sleepy, as it does in so many over-comfortable performances of earlier vintage (Teldec 3984-28144-2).

Twelve

1809
PIANO CONCERTO NO. 5 IN E FLAT MAJOR, OP. 73 ('EMPEROR')

Allegro   Adagio un poco mosso –   Rondo: Allegro

Beethoven did not intend the 'Emperor' to be his crowning piano concerto. Nor did he mean it to be one more tribute to Napoleon. The title was not his own, and he would have been surprised to know that that was how posterity, particularly in Britain, would identify his concerto in E flat major. Yet, as nicknames go, it was relevant to the martial, nowadays somewhat disconcerting, side of the music, just as it would have been relevant to the unfinished sixth piano concerto, if the surviving fragments of the first movement are anything to go by. But whether Beethoven's 'heroic' style – as heard in the 'Waldstein' and 'Appassionata' sonatas as well as in the 'Eroica' symphony and 'Emperor' concerto – was also a 'Napoleonic' style remains debatable. It is certainly something which the new wave of Beethoven performers tends to underplay.

Yet there is no doubt that, when Beethoven composed his fifth and biggest piano concerto in 1809, Napoleon was much on his mind. 'What a disturbing life around me: nothing but drums, cannons, soldiers, disasters of all sorts', he scribbled in response to the occupation of Vienna by Napoleon's troops. In such a context, the work's nickname, though frowned upon by Sir Donald Tovey, seems perfectly suitable. There is an imperial splendour about the orchestra's series of opening chords, each of them unleashing a torrential piano solo. From its very first note, the music continues the innovations in concerto form previously made in the Fourth Piano Concerto, itself more imperial than it is traditionally made out to be. By now, Beethoven was one step further away from the concerto as Mozart knew it. In Mozart's concertos, aggression was never allowed to disrupt the surface good manners of the music, no matter what was simmering beneath. In Beethoven's last completed concerto, aggression does break through, and the future of the concerto as a purveyor of conflict and resolution was thereby established.

After the preliminary trial of strength between Beethoven's protagonists at the start of the first movement, the orchestra proceeds to deliver the somewhat military – some might say deliberately hard-edged – main theme, which is succeeded by a chain of contrasted, clearly defined subsidiary melodies. The most important of these is played by soft, staccato strings in the minor, repeated smoothly, and to wonderful effect, by the horns in the major. When the piano re-enters, surprisingly quietly, it is with a chromatic scale, a trill and a decorated version of the main theme. But in the course of a taut central section, the forces are pitted more strenuously against each other, sometimes exploding in a giant burst of octaves, of a sort later composers would copy, with piano and orchestra striding in different directions. When the cadenza is reached, it comes with another Beethoven innovation – for, instead of being left traditionally to the soloist's powers of invention, it is scrupulously written out and ultimately dovetailed into a reappearance of the staccato theme, in which piano and horns are heard in combination.

After the ringing climax of the first movement, nothing could be more peaceful than the gentle, hymnlike beauty of the adagio in B major, though the idyllic simplicity of the main theme evidently cost Beethoven much trouble before he got it right. Apart from the dreamily descending triplets with which the soloist enters, the movement is devoted entirely to the opening melody, which on each repetition is bathed in different, ever more delicate light.

Then, in order to regain the key of E flat major and to usher in the finale, Beethoven delivers one of his harmonic masterstrokes – the bassoons, which have been holding the adagio's keynote of B, softly drop a semitone to B flat, which happens to be an important note in the home key. The horns join in, while the piano slowly gropes its way towards what will become the robust main theme of the finale. Robust, yes, in its resemblance to a traditional hunting motif of a sort found in Haydn and Mozart, but rhythmically intricate, not to say deliberately distorted in the way Beethoven chooses to accent it.

Once it has been established by soloist and orchestra – who in some performances inadvertently add distortions of their own – the music proceeds as a vigorous, elaborate rondo. An emphatically swinging dotted rhythm, prophetic of the first movement of the Seventh Symphony, plays an important part (Schumann, wanting to symbolise heroism, quoted it conspicuously in the finale of *Carnival*). Towards the close, this rhythm is tapped out for seventeen bars by the kettledrums, quietly underlining the work's military connections, while the soloist plays gradually fading chords. But just as the music reaches vanishing point, the players rally and bring the concerto to a resounding close.

Beethoven himself never played the 'Emperor' concerto in public. Popular theory declares that he was by then too deaf to do so; but in fact his priorities were changing. His career as a composer was what now mattered most to him, along with his determination to ensure that his works were accurately published, sometimes (as in the case of the Fourth Piano Concerto) even before they were publicly performed. The man who had been the greatest pianist of his period was now very definitely the greatest composer.

Though the 'Emperor' is played too often for its own good, Pierre-Laurent Aimard and Nikolaus Harnoncourt, in their recording released in the spring of 2003, rethought the work in its entirety and took no aspect of it on trust. The result is a performance of uncommon intelligence and truthfulness, creating, as one critic has put it, a sense of exploratory quest. There is no other recording in any way like it. The heroic side of the music emerges as something volatile and quirky, not so much heroic as simply dangerous. Only in the slow movement, though it is never dragged, is there any sense of repose. It is an entirely original, and very Beethovenian, approach to the work, well worth the cost of acquiring the whole, greatly fascinating three-disc set (Teldec Classics 0927 47334-2).

Unlike some other complete recordings, this one is completely unified and consistent in approach. Among performances available on a single disc, Murray Perahia's with Bernard Haitink and the Amsterdam Concertgebouw Orchestra, which also includes the Fourth Piano Concerto, has already been recommended. Alfred Brendel's with Sir Simon Rattle and the Vienna Philharmonic is enjoyably quizzical, the big bravura passages approached, or so you would think, with eyebrows raised. Without a coupling, the disc provides rather short measure (Philips 468 666-2). But a somewhat cheaper alternative lies in Brendel's older (1977) but no less satisfying recording of the same work, which does have a coupling in the form of a grandly spontaneous performance of the Choral Fantasia with Brendel as pianist.

NOTES ON BEETHOVEN

The orchestra is the London Philharmonic, the conductor Haitink (Philips 434 148-2).

Thirteen

1811
PIANO TRIO IN B FLAT MAJOR, OP. 97
('ARCHDUKE')

Allegro moderato

Andante cantabile, ma però con moto –

Scherzo: Allegro

Allegro moderato

The 'Archduke', the last of Beethoven's six piano trios, owes its nickname to his friend and pupil, the Archduke Rudolph, to whom it was dedicated. Like most of its predecessors, it is structured on a broad, four-movement plan, and has a high expressiveness, particularly in its slow movement, which has been thought in recent years to point towards his mysterious 'Immortal Beloved', now known to have been the Viennese-born Antonie Brentano, one of Beethoven's closest friends of the period.

Though domiciled in Frankfurt, where her husband was a merchant, she had returned to Vienna from 1809 until 1812 after the death of her father. Painstaking research by Maynard Solomon, the greatest of

Beethoven's biographers, produced overwhelming evidence in the 1970s of their secret liaison, resulting in the famous love letter of which she was the intended recipient. By the time the work received its long-delayed premiere in 1814, she had returned with her family to Germany.

By then, the composer's hearing had gone into a further decline, and the performance, with Ignaz Schuppanzigh and Joseph Linke as his distinguished partners, marked one of his last public appearances as pianist. According to the composer Ludwig Spohr, who was present, there was scarcely anything left of Beethoven's former virtuosity. 'In loud passages', he reported, 'the poor deaf man pounded on the keys till the strings jangled, and in quiet ones he played so softly that whole groups of notes were omitted, so that the music was unintelligible.'

Yet to what extent Spohr's reaction was provoked by Beethoven's deafness, and to what extent by the unusualness of some of the music itself, particularly in the scherzo, is hard to say. The piano's dynamic range in this work is, even by Beethoven's standards, uncommonly wide, and could well have shocked the ears of a Spohr. The work is remarkable in other ways, too, for it contains what the musical essayist, Donald Francis Tovey, perceptively called an 'integration of Mozart's and Haydn's resources, with results that transcend all possibility of resemblance to the style of their origins'.

For many people, the 'Archduke' is simply the greatest of all piano trios. Its spaciousness is suggested by the speed indications for the first movement and finale, both marked to be performed no faster than Allegro moderato. The whole work runs to a total of 1,200 bars, nearly 300 more than the quite substantial E flat major Trio, Op. 70, No. 2, which preceded it. The piano's big opening theme predicts the scale of the work to follow. The second subject, also introduced by the pianist, moves into the unexpected key of G major, with a resemblance to the music of the Fourth Piano Concerto, also written in that key. Much of the work, indeed, is quite grand and concerto-like, with scale passages reminiscent of the 'Emperor' concerto, completed two years previously. Yet the first movement remains pure chamber music, and one of the most stirring moments is the way, after mysterious trills and chromaticisms, the recapitulation starts with a magnificent new version of the main theme on the piano.

The scherzo, which comes second in the scheme of movements in the 'Archduke', opens with some skittish interplay between cello and violin, with the piano taking up the theme at the seventeenth bar. The central trio section contains shadowy chromatic passages – bordering, as one perceptive authority has pointed out, on Schoenbergian atonality, something still far in the future – interrupted by the pianist with a crashing dance-tune which subsides into little dancing motifs. After a reprise of the scherzo, there is a coda based on the chromaticisms of the central trio section.

The slow movement, much more expansive, opens with one of Beethoven's great lyrical melodies, sung first by the piano before forming the basis of a set of variations. These gain in richness and intensity as they proceed, until in the end the theme returns in new colours. Gradually the vision fades, and the finale follows without a break, the key side-slipping from the D major of the slow movement to the perky, almost polka-like main theme of the closing rondo in the home key of B flat major. Even here, however, B flat is by no means settled – and at one point, with a change of time and an increase in speed, Beethoven jerks the music into a completely alien key, and the rondo theme dances along in a racy new rhythm.

The 'Archduke' carries a special aura because it was Beethoven's final work in the form, and thus the 'deliberate' and 'unsurpassable' culmination of his output of piano trios. Such reputations among last works, however, usually need to be treated cautiously – and that of the 'Archduke' is no exception. In fact, Beethoven never intended it to be his last trio, and by 1816 he had embarked on another, in F minor, for the three children of his pianist friend, Marie Erdody. Work was proceeding well, as his sketchbooks confirm, when the composer heard that Marie's young son, August, had died suddenly after being struck on the head by his tutor. The new trio was abandoned and replaced by the refurbishment of a set of variations for piano trio he had written many years earlier. Though hardly substantial enough to cap the 'Archduke', the *Kakadu* variations, as they are known, are by no means insignificant. Indeed, in their rewritten form, they live up to their high opus number (Op. 121a).

For a recording which has the measure of the 'Archduke', the Beaux Arts Trio's is the one to turn to. Not only does the performance have beauty, dignity and spaciousness, but it forms part of a five-disc set which includes not only all the full-length trios but also a variety of fascinating odds and ends. Among these are the above-mentioned *Kakadu* variations, witty, polished, yet with more than a dash of emotional ambiguity. They are quite wonderfully played (Philips 468 411-2).

Fourteen

1812
Symphony No. 7 in A major, Op. 92

Poco sostenuto – Vivace   Allegretto

Presto   Allegro con brio

Wagner, in tribute to the relentless rhythmic vitality of Beethoven's Seventh Symphony, hailed it as the apotheosis of the dance. The same, with more justification, could be said about Stravinsky's *Rite of Spring*, since it was genuinely meant to be dance music, even though it now enjoys a predominantly concert-hall existence. Separated from each other by exactly 100 years, each work could be called the rhythmic *ne plus ultra* of its time. The *Rite* caused a riot in Paris in 1913. But the premiere of the Seventh Symphony in Vienna in 1813 provoked people to say that Beethoven must have been drunk when he wrote it.

It formed the tumultuous symphonic climax of his 'middle period', to which the fourth and fifth piano concertos and his previous symphonies from the 'Eroica' onwards also belonged. Beethoven, the greatest but most self-tortured composer of his time, could by then face his mounting deafness head-on, confident in his ability to master chaos and achieve through experience a new musical order. But if *Fidelio* and the Fifth Symphony were, in this respect, the most symbolic of his utterances, his Seventh Symphony fastened instead upon one powerful element of his musical make-up and hammered at it so obsessively that his sanity began to be questioned.

Of all Beethoven's works, this is the one in which we can visualise him most clearly tearing pages, knocking over ink-wells and (as neighbours complained) bellowing out the themes that rattled in his head. Big, modern symphony orchestras, with their lush string tone, seldom fully convey the sheer abrasiveness of this music. Smaller orchestras in smaller halls, with keen-edged woodwind, brazen horns, and kettledrums which can cut fiercely through the fabric of the strings, give a better impression of what the first performance must have been like. On that occasion, in a programme which additionally contained Beethoven's ceremonial and (at the time) wildly successful *Battle Symphony*, the unstoppable verve of the Seventh Symphony, exhilarating yet awesome, prompted people to assume that it, too, must have been inspired by Napoleonic defeat and the promise of European peace. Indeed, the concert in which it was performed, after Napoleon's retreat from Moscow, was for the benefit of Austrian and Bavarian soldiers wounded at the Battle of Hanau.

In itself, however, it is never peaceful music. There is hardly a moment when the work is at rest. Even the slow movement, significantly marked *allegretto* rather than *andante* or *adagio*, proceeds with a steady tread, based on a repeated dactylic rhythm which shifts from section to section of the orchestra and of which the composer refuses to let go. Each of the four movements, indeed, has its own dominating pulse. Like the Fifth Symphony, the Seventh is a study in the use of powerfully circling motion, which had also been a strenuous feature of the first movement of the second 'Razumovsky' string quartet.

The big (but never heavy) chords that launch the first movement, followed by repeatedly rising scales for the strings that will ferociously return towards the end of the finale, create an impression of size and grandeur, though the Seventh is by no means the longest of Beethoven's symphonies. Nor, in spite of its ferocity, is it the most lavishly scored. The orchestral forces required are smaller than those of at least four of his other symphonies, but they are possessed by a frenzy of a sort found nowhere else in his music – except in the Eighth Symphony, a still shorter, more genial, but at times even more volcanic work.

The fierce revolving nature of the Seventh Symphony dominates three of the four movements, and is audible even in the depths of the allegretto, the one portion of the work in which it is not loudly to the fore. The main *vivace* section of the first movement shows what is in store. The swinging dotted rhythm of the main theme acts like a dynamo that is never switched off. At one point, it quietly heaves and seethes in the cellos and basses, even when the other players are momentarily trying to produce music more sustained (this famous passage, towards the end of the movement, was the one that supposedly prompted Weber, who should have known better, to declare Beethoven to be ripe for the madhouse). And it erupts again, with whooping horns, in the movement's closing pages.

After the major-key brilliance of the first movement, the minor-key melancholy of the succeeding allegretto inevitably sounds funereal, though not to the extent that it becomes a rerun of the apocalyptic funeral march in the 'Eroica'. The pace, for a start, is too fast – or should be, if the conductor knows what he is doing – even though the structure is similar to that of the great *marcia funebre* in the 'Eroica' symphony. There is solemnity here, and restlessness, rather than grief. The middle section, with its clarinet melody, is wistful. But the pulse is what matters, and it underpins every change of mood or colour.

In the scherzo, the fast spinning motion resumes. Since this is one of Beethoven's extended scherzos with two trio sections (and even, at the very end, a brief attempt to launch a third one), repetition is strongly emphasised. The rhythms continue to pound and swing, even in the glowing music of the trio if it is played fast enough and the bottom notes on the horns are properly audible. Finally, five whiplash chords sever the continuity. But in the finale, hailed by Tovey as a 'triumph of Bacchic fury', it immediately resumes. Here, in the ceaseless interplay of short repeated motifs and longer repeated sections, we are made more than ever aware of Beethoven's obsessiveness, until the music hurtles wildly into the abyss.

From Felix Weingartner onwards, there have been many excellent recordings of the Seventh Symphony. On the conductor's part, it is not, after all, a work which lies open to serious misinterpretation. Crisp rhythms, fleet speeds and transparent textures are what count, and Sir John Eliot Gardiner achieves them to admiration with the incisive period instrumentalists of his London-based Orchestre Révolutionnaire et Romantique. A rip-roaring account of the Eighth Symphony, a work many conductors are content to emasculate, serves as the ideal pendant (DG Archiv 447 063-2).

If this all sounds more exhausting than exhilarating – though the slow movement of the Seventh, never overpressed, achieves a poise and poignancy rare in Gardiner – Toscanini's cleaned-up 1936 recording with the New York Philharmonic is hardly the alternative. Coupled with an equally formidable Fifth Symphony, this is Beethoven as a battering-ram (Naxos 8 110840). Carlos Kleiber comes closer to true exhilaration in his coupling of the same two works with the Vienna Philharmonic (DG 447 400-2), and Sir Roger Norrington's performance with the London Classical Players is refreshingly light-toned. The coupling is a racy, witty account of the Fourth Symphony, not a self-consciously 'great' performance but a thoroughly attractive and spirited one (Virgin Veritas VMS 61376-2).

Fifteen

1814
FIDELIO, OP. 72

Opera in two acts

Beethoven's one and only opera has always divided its public. For those who love it, who carry it in their souls from one performance to the next, it is the masterpiece of masterpieces. To suggest to these people that, like any other opera, it may have its faults is to meet with frowns of bafflement. *Fidelio* is not like any other opera. It stands apart, beyond criticism, its greatness self-evident and indisputable. Why, then, are there listeners who get nothing out of it at all, who pour scorn on its plot, and hold convictions which, however wrong, are as sincere as those of its admirers?

The answers of the anti-*Fidelio* faction come easily. For a start, they claim that the heroic wife who is the central character seems an unbelievable fantasy on the part of a man who knew nothing about being married and whose vision of conjugal love was unrealistically idealistic. What, they inquire, will happen to Leonore and Florestan after the curtain falls? Since the same question could be asked more pertinently about the lovers in Mozart's *Così fan tutte*, an opera Beethoven despised, it seems hardly relevant to his vision of *Fidelio*.

But, they add, is there not something seriously wrong with the theatrical consistency of a work which begins as a traditional German comedy, develops into the most tense and moving of music dramas, and ends as a cantata? Does the very fact that Beethoven took more than a decade to compose it, wrote three versions of it, and supplied it with four overtures, not reek of indecision? Working for the first time in the world of opera, the man clearly did not know what he was doing, and never got it right.

As someone whose first indelible encounter with *Fidelio* was in Günther Rennert's stark Hamburg production brought to the Edinburgh Festival soon after the Second World War, I admit to a prickle of irritation whenever one of its detractors blandly dismisses it in such terms. It is then, it seems to me, that the difference between liking and disliking a work is not merely a matter of opposite standpoints but a question of understanding and misunderstanding. If you understand *Fidelio*, you love it. If you love it, you commit yourself to it. The matter is as simple as that. As a critic, I have always avoided writing in the first person about music; but there are some works which make it seem necessary. *Fidelio* is one of them.

Beethoven toyed with the idea of other operas in the course of his career. Sketches for *Macbeth* found their way into his 'Ghost' trio, Op. 70, No. 1.

His interest in Goethe's *Faust* never yielded the opera, or even the incidental music, which many people longed for. It was *Fidelio* which consumed him, and tormented him, from the moment he first encountered it, in French, and recognised it as his operatic destiny.

The text, under the name of *Leonore, or Conjugal Love*, had been written in the 1790s by Jean-Nicolas Bouilly, governor of an area of the Loire during the period of terror which followed the French Revolution. It was said to have been based (like Mozart's *Così fan tutte*) on an actual incident, involving in this case a brave young wife who, disguised as a man, had gained access to her husband's prison and helped him to escape. If the story is true, then Bouilly has gained immortality by being the real-life Don Fernando, the humane minister who in the closing scene of Beethoven's opera sets Florestan free and reunites him with Leonore.

Cherubini, resident in Paris, was the composer of heroic, revolutionary operas who served as Beethoven's model. Ferdinando Paer, another Paris resident, had in 1805 written an opera on the subject, which showed Beethoven what was possible. But whereas Paer's opera was competent, Beethoven's was sublime – even if, at its original premiere in the same year as Paer's, it still had a long way to go.

Where it went, between then and 1814, was through a cutting and refining process of inspired ruthlessness, which stripped away every unnecessary note or word. Even *Abscheulicher!* ('Monster!'), Leonore's great Act One statement of faith and hope in the face of oppression, was reduced by almost half. What could be cut to the bone was duly cut. But did Beethoven in the end wield the knife too brutally? A beautiful passage recently restored by Sir Charles Mackerras to the closing scene suggests that he may have done. As Beethoven himself felt compelled to put it: 'Of all my children, this was born in greatest labour.'

But the effort, as the 1814 performance disclosed, was worth it. The music had gone through fire and emerged finely tempered. The original version, under the title of *Leonore*, remains a fascinating unedited draft. It was Beethoven's relentless assault on his own music which transformed it into the searing experience it ultimately became.

No recording of *Fidelio* is perfect, but Nikolaus Harnoncourt's gets so much of it so superbly and passionately right that searching for something better seems futile. In terms of pace, rhythm and articulation, it has all it needs, and more than it usually gets. The classical Mozartian basis of the music, the touches of *The Magic Flute* and *Die Entführung* upon which Beethoven builds his mighty superstructure, is perceptively caught. The music never strains to be something other than it is. The characters — Charlotte Margiono's Leonore, Peter Seiffert's Florestan, Sergei Leiferkus's Don Pizarro and Barbara Bonney's Marzelline — are real people, not symbols of courage, sweetness, tenderness, compassion, ambivalence or evil.

The Chamber Orchestra of Europe has the correct Beethovenian scale, which does not mean too big a sound, but certainly means incisiveness — along with (essential in this work) the most vivid oboe-playing from the heartfelt Douglas Boyd. Likewise, the professional voices of the Arnold Schoenberg Choir have a finesse and precision of expression which go beyond what is usually heard in performances of *Fidelio*. The drama is made to sound as unified and unstoppable, the dungeon scene as dark and hollow-toned, as Beethoven in his final version of the score had battled to make it (Teldec 4509-94560-2).

Three other recordings possess the special qualities for which the music cries out. Otto Klemperer's, with Christa Ludwig and Jon Vickers as heroine and hero, is old but famously persuasive (EMI CMS5 67364-2); Ferenc Fricsay's, with Dietrich Fischer-Dieskau as villain, is even older but marvellously alive and a great bargain (DG 453 106-2); and Sir Charles Mackerras's, based on a concert performance with the Scottish Chamber Orchestra at the Edinburgh Festival, is keenly alert to the pace of the drama and to the fine detail of Beethovenian style (Telarc CD 80439).

Sixteen

1816
AN DIE FERNE GELIEBTE, OP. 98

Song cycle

Not many singers champion Beethoven's songs. Dietrich Fischer-Dieskau, before his retirement, was one who did, and he memorably devoted an entire evening to them at the 1970 Edinburgh Festival's celebration of the composer's 200th birthday. Since then, however, the position has not greatly changed. All the old misconceptions – that Beethoven's songs are less memorably melodious than Schubert's, that they are too difficult to sing, that nobody knows them, that there are not enough of them to compile a programme from, that they pre-date the invention of the German *Lied* (or 'art-song') – continue to exist and carry weight.

Beethoven's father and grandfather were singers, but Beethoven himself, according to friends who listened to him, could only growl or howl. Yet he composed about 100 songs (not counting the tedious folk-song arrangements which he and Haydn poured out for the voracious George Thomson of Edinburgh). Many of them are hauntingly melodious, sharply characterised, rich in subject matter, pungently humorous as well as lyrical, amorous, touching, pastoral, macabre, philosophical and religious, and for the most part still surprisingly unfamiliar. As Fischer-Dieskau confirmed, they are capable of sustaining an entire programme; but what we usually have to make do with is a token group of them at the start of a recital, because that is considered the place to put 'early' songs. Though it is hard to imagine Beethoven being crowded out by anyone else, this is what Schubert, Schumann, Brahms, Wolf and Strauss have combined to do to him.

For many people, Beethoven's vocal writing begins and ends with the splendours of the Ninth Symphony and the *Missa Solemnis*, grand, hugely demanding works which give a false impression of what his songs might be like. In fact, they are as intimate and personal, often as epigrammatic, as his piano bagatelles – though these, too, are infrequently performed in public. They are also suggestive of passages in his chamber music which get described as 'songlike', because Beethoven was always attuned to the art of *bel canto*, as his solo violin and cello lines, and the slow movements of his piano sonatas, frequently disclose.

Songs, like sonatas and string quartets, were a natural part of his output. He wrote songs during his adolescence in Bonn and at the height of his fame in Vienna. He wrote them in times of illness and stress. He found kindred spirits in Goethe and Gellert. He composed German songs and Italian songs – and one of his amorous Italian songs, to words by Metastasio, exists in alternative comic and serious versions, which need to be placed side by side to make their full effect. Songs, in other words, were a stimulus to him.

But *An die ferne Geliebte* ('To the Distant Loved One') is more than a song, more ambitious, more daring – and utterly original, in that it is in fact a song cycle, the first of its kind by a major composer. Written in 1816, it not only pre-dates Schubert's *Die schöne Müllerin*, traditionally hailed as the first-ever song cycle, but it approaches the idea of a unified set of songs in its own, entirely different, way. Unity, as Beethoven perceived it, meant actually linking the songs and their piano accompaniments together, so that the six songs could be heard, if the listener felt inclined, as a long and episodic single one.

Beethoven's innovations, however, went further than that. By ending *An die ferne Geliebte* with the music that had opened it, he composed what was, in effect, the first cyclic song cycle. It was something Schubert never did, but which Schumann, who knew the Beethoven cycle intimately, would later do in two of his own song cycles. Whether Beethoven himself ever thought of it as a cycle is debatable. In the year of its composition, the form had not been identified by name, and it could be that Beethoven regarded *An die ferne Geliebte* as a substantial single song in several sections, totalling about fifteen minutes. Schubert would later compose many such songs, some of them even longer, and it seems likely that that was how the work's first listeners must have heard it.

Did they think it was inspired by some personal incident in Beethoven's life? That was another matter altogether. Beethoven, like Schubert, composed many songs of longing for unspecified beloveds, though the scale, intensity, poignancy and striking originality of *An die ferne Geliebte* may suggest it to represent something uncommonly close to his heart – or, as Schumann put it when he came to write his C major Fantasy for solo piano (quoting a strain from *An die ferne Geliebte* in the process) that his work was a 'deep lament' for his beloved but absent Clara, his future wife.

For Beethoven, there was no future wife. His lament, if it was for anybody at all, remains a mystery. Modern detection, however, suggests that it was in memory of his unnamed 'Immortal Beloved', now identified as Antonie Brentano, who had moved from Vienna in the winter of 1812, leaving Beethoven so bereft, it would seem, that his musical output seriously faltered for several years, before reviving with new intensity.

So, what is the truth about *An die ferne Geliebte*? As a song cycle to words by a minor poet, Alois Jeitteles, it may simply be a generalised expression of love and despair. But bearing in mind the distant presence of Antonie Brentano – to whom, significantly, Beethoven gave the autograph manuscript of a different song, simply entitled 'An die Geliebte' ('To the Beloved') – the six sections of the work and their obsessively cyclic structure could carry a more precise message. Heard as the musical embodiment of Beethoven's famous, greatly moving and unposted letter to his Immortal Beloved, its effect is overwhelming.

Happily, Dietrich Fischer-Dieskau's beautifully phrased, meticulously articulated, wholly unsentimentalised interpretation of it, with Joerg Demus as pianist, has been preserved on disc as part of Deutsche Grammophon's collected edition of Beethoven's works. All the other fine songs, performed by a variety of responsive singers and pianists, are in this reduced-price three-disc box, including those to sacred texts by Christian Gellert and the two grieving, questioning, death-conscious settings of Christoph Tiedge's 'An die Hoffnung' ('To Hope'), again with Fischer-Dieskau at his most eloquent (DG 453 782-2). And, of course, the tender little 'An die Geliebte'.

Alternatively, on a more recent but full-price single disc, the young baritone Stephan Genz gives an exemplary account of *An die ferne Geliebte* and other Beethoven songs, partnered by Roger Vignoles and greatly recommended (Hyperion CDA67055).

Seventeen

1822
PIANO SONATA IN C MINOR, OP. 111

Maestoso – Allegro con brio ed appassionato
Arietta: Adagio molto semplice e cantabile

Beethoven's thirty-second and last piano sonata remains one of the great musical challenges for performers, its presence in his output like that of a mountain range visible from afar and growing more ominous the closer one gets to it. Even its opus number inspires a certain frisson of awe. Its opening notes stop you in your tracks, which was surely Beethoven's intention. Not even the mighty *Hammerklavier* sonata, that Everest of a work completed four years earlier, contains anything as threatening as those terse opening notes in C minor, and their thunderous progress into the succeeding Allegro con brio, the music filled with suggestions of cliff faces, chasms, torrents and avalanches. As Alfred Brendel, not a pianist who tends to speak picturesquely about music, has said of this sonata:

'there are subterranean sounds and stratospheric sounds either veiled in cloud or floating on high with crystalline clarity'. Though some people, more simply, see the work as a contrast between Earth and Heaven, Brendel's description could hardly be bettered.

Perhaps it is C minor, Beethoven's famously dramatic key, that does it. Yet its sound here is quite different from that of the Piano Trio, Op. 1, No. 3, or the Third Piano Concerto, or the Fifth Symphony, though the first movement of the 'Pathétique' sonata provides a distant glimpse of what lay ahead. Essentially, however, it belongs in its own world, which is that of the last triptych of sonatas, in which elements of fugue and variation form are fused and transfigured at the keyboard in Beethoven's own way. The fact that the instrument involved is Beethoven's own one, even though it was years since he had played it in public, speaks for itself. It is impossible to imagine the work being performed by anything else.

As a great keyboard improviser, Beethoven in his youth had employed variation form as a natural vehicle for his prowess. His first known work, dating from 1782, was a set of nine keyboard variations on a march by Ernst Christoph Dressler. His *Eroica Variations*, written twenty years later, were a milestone in the development of his piano style, and so were the C minor variations that followed. By the time he was 50, he had written more than sixty sets of variations of one kind or another; but those that close his piano sonatas Op. 109 and Op. 111, along with the huge set of

Diabelli variations which capped his career as a composer for the piano, reveal his command of the form at its most cogent.

In the two years that separated Op. 109 and Op. 111, Beethoven had thought afresh about sonata layout, with the result that Op. 111 consists not of the usual three or four movements but of only two. Yet this does not make the sonata a short one, except by the standards of the *Hammerklavier*, nor does it sound in any way unfinished. Charles Rosen, in his book on classical style, refers to its expansiveness by calling the second movement a study in suspended harmonic motion, with almost quarter of an hour of the purest C major before there is a marked change of key. But though this may give some idea of the scale of the work, the music also has a characteristic Beethovenian terseness. The two movements have a perfection of balance and contrast that justifies the claim that Beethoven here set the limits of the piano sonata in amplitude of conception, perfection of design, vigour of movement and rightness of detail.

In its progress from C minor to C major, it follows a route very different from that of the Fifth Symphony. The first half of the work begins and ends in C minor, the second begins and ends in C major. In no sense is there a contest between the two keys, or an element of transition, or any suggestion that the ending is a triumph of light over darkness. The two movements – two metaphysical slabs of Beethoven – are simply juxtaposed, the one the obverse, as well as the resolution, of the other.

NOTES ON BEETHOVEN

From initial ground plan to final masterpiece, Beethoven's last sonata underwent changes so radical that it emerged a wholly different work. Not even the key of C minor was a premeditated aspect of its design. Yet, once he had hit on the idea of contrast – between two movements, two keys, two areas of the keyboard – he was on the way to achieving the dramatic entity he was looking for. His efforts paid off. The C minor first movement, with Bach as its fountainhead, is a faultless example of the welding of fantasy, fugue and sonata form which preoccupied him in his later years.

The slow introduction, with its initial downward plunge of not quite an octave (the span known as a diminished seventh), strikes like a thunderclap. Resounding chords, trills and modulations sustain the sense of disruption. The rumbling transition to the main Allegro con brio section reverberates like an earthquake through the depths of the piano. Beethoven's deafness in no way inhibited his musical imagination, and he was now exploring and attacking the extremes of the piano's by then extended keyboard in a manner even more audacious than before. To hear this music is to understand how Beethoven was capable of maltreating his servants and (reputedly) of pouring a sub-standard stew over the head of the waiter who served it.

With its stormy semiquaver passages, its moments when the skies briefly lighten, and its restless closing bars which surely, a decade later, inspired Chopin's *Revolutionary* study in the same key, this movement might seem the essence of nineteenth-century romanticism. Yet it is firmly grounded in the art of fugue (the development section, indeed, is a double fugue), and the chords that opened the slow introduction play an important structural role in the movement as a whole. The music is a triumph of form as well as content.

The second movement is a sublime synthesis of slow movement and finale. It opens, like the finale of Op. 109, with a theme of the calmest beauty, whose unusual and intricate time signature (nine semiquavers in the bar, scrupulously devised by a composer notoriously ignorant of arithmetic) serves to give the music its special breadth and flow. But while the harmony hangs suspended in C major, the variations gain in rhythmic intensity and complexity as they proceed, exploiting memorable effects of light and shade, height and depth, and at one point of almost jazzy syncopation, until the music reaches what Tovey called an 'ecstatic' vision.

The publisher who asked Beethoven if he had forgotten to send him the finale was acting in the belief that sonatas in Beethoven's day had three or four movements, not just two, and that the finale was often something light and brief. It was an understandable assumption, though he should have known that Beethoven had done this sort of thing before. But, in bringing the second movement full circle to something like its starting point, Beethoven created his own statement of finality. It might not have worked so well in an earlier sonata. It certainly worked in this one, and in so doing it made history. The closing notes, played *pianissimo*, are brief –

no more than a short note followed by a shorter one, or, in musical parlance, a quaver followed by a semiquaver. 'The modesty of the final chord', says Charles Rosen, 'is significant.'

The obvious way to buy a recording of Beethoven's last sonata is as part of the final triptych; but Brendel and Rosen, by placing it in the context of the last six sonatas, provide a better option – and at bargain price. Brendel, in his recent conversation book, warns against making music sound too beautiful, and he certainly applies no cosmetics to Op. 111. It is the inner beauty he captures, particularly in the slow movement, along with the work's rigour, quirkiness and irascibility (Philips Duo 438 374-2). The last three sonatas are also available on a single disc (Philips 446 701-2).

Rosen's performance, rather more severe, may miss some of Brendel's humanity and sense of the work's strangeness, yet is no less impressive. His command of the finale, at a pace which never loses the music's impulse, is undeviating (Sony SB2K 53531). Each pianist's triple trills – as Beethoven's own must once have been – are a tour de force. The inclusion of the *Hammerklavier* sonata in both sets, and in very different performances, is a massive bonus, not least because Brendel, at the age of 70, gave up playing this finger-wrenching and memory-challenging work in public. Though neither set is new, the sound quality has lost nothing in immediacy. Nor has that of three other performances of Op. 111, by Wilhelm Backhaus, Claudio Arrau and Paul Badura Skoda, which have the advantage of being issued on one single disc. Not merely for those who enjoy comparisons, these performances gain an extra fascination through being given on three different makes of piano.

The excitable Backhaus's responsive Bechstein may be the winner for some listeners, especially anyone who recalls him playing in post-war Vienna, where (according to Brendel) he was considered to be Beethoven personified. But Arrau, on what sounds like a massive Steinway, brings armour-plated weight to the music, and Badura Skoda on his Bosendorfer brings the music as close as it can get to Viennese brightness and warmth (Aura 113-2 ADD).

Eighteen

1822
MISSA SOLEMNIS IN D MAJOR, OP. 123

Kyrie   Gloria   Credo   Sanctus   Benedictus   Agnus Dei

Of the four great large-scale masses of the nineteenth century, three were requiems written by non-believers. The fourth, and earliest, was Beethoven's *Missa Solemnis*, written by a composer who undoubtedly believed in God but whose religious attitudes were his own and as non-conformist as his responses to everything else. To the more orthodox Haydn, whose six superb symphonic masses written between 1796 and 1802 were direct precursors of the *Missa Solemnis*, Beethoven was an atheist – though one, as he put it, who had 'several heads, several hearts and several souls'. One of Beethoven's own remarks, that 'Jesus was only a poor human being and a Jew', nearly brought about his excommunication.

Martin Cooper, in his investigative study of Beethoven's last decade, declared that 'If Beethoven's beliefs are hard to discover, the prayers or *cris de cœur* – there is no other word for them – make it clear that his religious feelings were strong'. It is evidence confirmed by his music itself, not only by the *Missa Solemnis* (Berlioz's *Grand Messe des Morts*, Brahms's *German Requiem* and Verdi's *Manzoni Requiem*, after all, sound equally devout) but also by the 'Heiliger Dankgesang' from the A minor String Quartet, Op. 132, in which Beethoven hymned his thanks to God for his recovery from serious illness. Further testimony is provided by the 'Pastoral' symphony (where every tree, according to the composer, says 'Holy, holy!' and the finale is a solemn hymn of thanksgiving for improved weather), by the finale of the Ninth Symphony (where God is hailed as the father in whom all men are brothers), and by many a God-conscious slow movement.

All this may suggest that the increasingly deaf and inward-turning Beethoven was more interested in a religion of his own than in one based on specific Christian doctrine. The *Missa Solemnis*, as he said, was written 'from the heart to the heart'. The personal side of the music is heard immediately in the hush of the Kyrie, a movement of extreme intimacy and simplicity; and it recurs in the serene Benedictus where, in one of the work's most famous passages, a solo violin meditates serenely on the words 'Blessed is He that cometh in the name of the Lord'. Though the sweetness of this music dismayed Martin Cooper, who deemed it embarrassingly sentimental, it is generally acknowledged to be one of the score's most haunting passages, and a vital part in Beethoven's conception of the work.

It was hardly the composer's fault if it seemed to anticipate the infamous 'Meditation' from *Thais*, Massenet's much-derided operatic mixture of sex and sanctimony. The true links of the 'Benedictus' are with Beethoven's own music – with the Violin Concerto, the two exquisite *Romances* for violin and orchestra, and the 'canon' quartet from *Fidelio*.

Beethoven composed his *Missa Solemnis* for his good friend and bene-factor, the Archduke Rudolph of Austria, to whom he also dedicated the 'Archduke' trio, his last two piano concertos, his *Les Adieux*, *Hammerklavier* and Opus 111 piano sonatas, his last violin sonata and the *Grosse Fuge* for string quartet – a very special friend indeed, then. Earlier in his career, he had produced other sacred music, including his fine C major Mass, an oratorio (*Christ on the Mount of Olives*) and several cantatas; but the *Missa Solemnis*, as Beethoven stated before he wrote it, was to be more important than any of these.

Its principal *raison d'être* was the election of Rudolph (a notable Beethoven pupil, pianist and composer who was too frail for a military career) as Archbishop of Olmutz in Moravia. In a letter, Beethoven told him that 'The day on which a High Mass of mine is performed at the solemnities for your Royal Highness will be the happiest of my life, and God will enlighten me so that my weak powers may contribute to the glorification of this solemn event'. Yet the *Missa Solemnis* was no routine 'royal' work, written to order. It was composed because Rudolph was Beethoven's friend, not because he was a wealthy archduke.

The composition, begun in 1818, was not completed until four years later. During that period, Beethoven characteristically worked on a variety of other projects as well, including the last three piano sonatas, the *Diabelli* variations and the grand neo-baroque concert overture, *The Consecration of the House*. As so often, his private life at the time was in startling contrast to the music he was creating. There is a famous anecdote by Anton Schindler, Beethoven's (unreliable) early biographer, who called on him one August afternoon in 1819 and found him in disarray. 'As soon as we entered,' he reported, 'we learned that in the morning both servants had gone away, and that there had been a quarrel after midnight which had disturbed all the neighbours, because as a consequence of a long vigil both had gone to sleep and the food which had been prepared had become uneatable.'

Nor was this all. 'In the living-room behind a door,' he continued, 'we heard the master sing parts of the fugue in the Credo – singing, howling, stamping. After we had been listening a long time to this awful scene, and were about to go away, the door opened and Beethoven stood before us with distorted features. He looked as if he had been in mortal combat with the whole host of contrapuntists, his everlasting enemies.'

Counterpoint, however, was by no means as uncongenial to Beethoven as Schindler implied, and in these last years of his life it was among the foundations of his entire musical thinking. Yet the sheer scale of this work was a challenge so great that Beethoven failed to complete it in time for its magisterial premiere. The first performance did not take place until 26 March 1824 in St Petersburg, where it was presented under the auspices of Prince Galitzin, Beethoven's Russian friend and patron.

By then, Beethoven had hawked this great late masterpiece round various performers; but the Russians were among the few who responded. Prior to the belated premiere, however, three movements of the mass were included in a concert in Vienna, when the Ninth Symphony was also performed and the conductor was Beethoven himself. The deaf composer, it is said, could hear neither the performance nor the applause, until at the end one of the soloists turned him round, and he was able to see the ovation he was receiving.

Has the performance of Beethoven's great Mass in the context for which it was initially conceived – liturgically, at the installation of a Royal Cardinal Archbishop – ever really been a feasibility? It has certainly been performed religiously at Westminster Abbey, as a Mass within a Mass; but, as one critic tartly observed, 'it was Beethoven who stole the show'. Willy Hess, in his edition of the miniature score, put it another way when he wrote that the insertion of liturgical units 'must have the effect of implanting foreign bodies into a unified organic work of art, and as such they will impair the overall musical and artistic impression'.

Of all Beethoven's works, the *Missa Solemnis* remains the most notoriously intimidating. There are good Beethoven conductors who fight shy of it and swear they will never perform it. Beethoven was unsparing in his demands on the voices of his singers, in the quantity and weight and difficulty of the music he gave them to sing, sometimes multisyllabically in their upper register, or else, equally dauntingly, in their bottom register. People say it was all because he was deaf, and therefore unaware of what he was imposing on his performers; but that is a ridiculous assumption. Beethoven did not need to hear what he was writing. It was all in his head. The most dramatic, and taxing, movements are the Gloria and Credo, and Beethoven knew perfectly well how difficult they were.

The Sanctus, on the other hand, is more intimate, more mysterious, characterised by soft-toned trombones; but there is a great, more outgoing moment when the words 'Pleni sunt coeli' ('Heaven and Earth are full of thy glory') interrupt the mood of rapt devotion. The Agnus Dei opens sombrely in B minor, but later moves into the work's home key of D major. The music is interrupted from time to time (very strikingly, though puritanical listeners regard it as a trivialisation) by the sound of military trumpets and drums, which may be meant as a memory of Napoleonic invasion – though equally it may have been inspired by Haydn's *Paukenmesse* ('Kettledrum Mass'). Like the martial music in the finale of the Ninth Symphony, the 'popular' elements amid the sublime, it is a reminder of Beethoven's humanity. It is also marvellous, greatly touching music, written by a composer who, at the age of 54, was already considered old. The *Missa Solemnis* is a work both worldly and other-worldly.

NOTES ON BEETHOVEN

For many years, the fine old Otto Klemperer recording, with Elisabeth Schwarzkopf heading its array of soloists, was the one considered to have the grandest grip upon the music. Among performances in the big old German tradition, it is still the one to go for. But most conductors today, recognising that the *Missa Solemnis* is not a lumbering pantechnicon, opt for lighter orchestral and choral forces, greatly to the work's advantage.

In Sir John Eliot Gardiner's performance with his Monteverdi Choir and Orchestre Révolutionnaire et Romantique, the use of period instruments never debilitates the music. With Charlotte Margiono, Catherine Robbin, William Kendall and Alastair Miles as soloists, this is a performance so sure, so dynamic and so exhilarating that you wonder how the work was ever considered difficult (DG Archiv 429 779-2). Contained on a single disc, this may seem a clear first choice.

Spread over two discs, Nikolaus Harnoncourt's rival recording with the Chamber Orchestra of Europe and Arnold Schoenberg Choir is a costly alternative; but the performance – more mellow, less 'heroic', not so aggressively recorded – has other things to offer. With speeds slightly slower than Gardiner's, it lasts ten minutes longer. But they are ten minutes well spent, enabling Harnoncourt to capture the spun-out sweetness of the music as well as its energy. Though he does not employ original instruments, he imposes a keen sense of period style on his responsive young players which, as in his other Beethoven recordings, proves just as rewarding. As soloists, Eva Mei, Marjana Lipovšek, Anthony Rolfe Johnson and Robert Holl sound as integrated as the rest of the performance (Teldec 0630-18945-2).

Nineteen

1824
SYMPHONY NO. 9 IN D MINOR, OP. 125

Allegro ma non troppo, un poco maestoso
Molto vivace – Presto – Tempo I
Adagio molto e cantabile – Andante moderato
Finale: *Ode to Joy*

Beethoven's ninth and last (or last completed) symphony was never called 'The Choral' by its composer, even though that was how generations of music-lovers came to know it. Beethoven himself preferred the longer and more accurate title 'Symphony with final chorus on Schiller's *Ode to Joy*', but today that would seem too much of a mouthful. To call it simply 'The Ninth', in fact, is sufficient to imply whose ninth is being referred to. It was the prototype of all the other great ninth symphonies – Dvořák's, Bruckner's and Mahler's, though Schubert's was really his eighth – which followed.

Fragments of what would become Beethoven's biggest, most complex and most ambitiously orchestrated symphony had been in his mind for years. As a boy in Bonn and young man in Vienna, he already knew Schiller's *Ode to Joy*. A startling foretaste of the symphony's opening theme can be found, in the same key, in the introduction to his Second Symphony, written in 1802. The *Choral Fantasia*, tacked on to the famous four-hour concert containing the premieres of the fifth and sixth symphonies at the Theater an der Wien in 1808, displayed the finale of the Ninth in embryonic form. A fugue subject, jotted in his notebook in 1815, found its way into the scherzo. The sound of military bands, heard by Beethoven during his walks in Vienna's Prater, where Orson Welles would later voice his opinion of Swiss cuckoo clocks in *The Third Man*, is reflected in the zing-boom of cymbals and drums in one episode of the finale.

Not until 1823, however, did composition of the Ninth begin in earnest. Beethoven's plan to write a purely orchestral finale, employing material later transferred to the A minor String Quartet, Op. 132, was swept aside by the masterstroke which was the *Ode to Joy*. To a friend, Beethoven reputedly exclaimed: 'I've got it'. By May 1824, the work was ready for its premiere in Vienna's Kärntnerthor Theatre, with seats for only 650 people (a reminder that the work was not conceived for a vast concert hall), but ample standing room. The deaf composer conducted it, or at any rate set the tempi, while a deputy held the performance together. Franz Schubert, aged 27, was in the audience.

The epic scale of the symphony, which Wagner would later find so inspirational when he came to write *The Ring* and other music dramas, is immediately suggested by the gradual mobilising and establishing of the first movement's main theme. The volcanic recapitulation, which erupts with a violence never heard in orchestral music before, not even in the first movement of the 'Eroica', shows how far Beethoven was now prepared to take symphonic form, and the sonorously funereal coda confirms the grandeur of the conception.

The succeeding scherzo, with its galvanising kettledrums, maintains the work's vast momentum. Not even the rustic trio section can slow things down – indeed, the pace grows even faster to *presto* – and only the arrival of the long-spun slow movement ultimately brings a sense of peace, treacherously difficult though it is to perform, and mysteriously interrupted though it is by the sound of slow fanfares across an empty landscape. With its two gloriously alternating themes and variations, however, and its atmosphere of hushed tenderness, the music could almost belong to one of Beethoven's last string quartets, which perhaps shows why his original ideas for the finale were so easily transferred to one of these works.

But the blaring, pounding discords of the finale's opening fanfare, bursting in on the serenity of the adagio, reassert the symphony's sweeping sense of orchestral drama and suspense. What is happening here? There are terse exclamations from the strings, suggestive of operatic recitative. There are brief quotations from the three preceding movements, each of them rudely interrupted, followed by a hint of something different – the theme of what will become the *Ode to Joy*.

The music is now finally on track. The unforgettable hymnlike theme, which has become modern Europe's great unifying international anthem (even if the participants in a British TV quiz once failed to recognise it, to the astonishment of Sir Georg Solti, who was present), is gradually unfurled and welcomed by a man's solo voice. The vocal portion of the finale has arrived, proclaiming Schiller's ode in the Beethovenian guise of a set of variations. These incorporate, with the endless resourcefulness of Beethoven at the height of his powers, a heroic march, a double fugue, an ecstatic slow section with the men's voices underpinned by trombones, a tribute to God (this was the period of Beethoven's *Missa Solemnis*), an exquisite cadenza for the solo quartet, and a coda frenzied in its climactic outpouring of joy.

Though it was destined to form the climax of Beethoven's symphonic output, the composer never saw his Ninth Symphony that way. By 1825, he was sketching his Tenth Symphony, a work which – like Mahler's Tenth, Bruckner's Ninth and Schubert's Tenth (more accurately his Ninth) – was never completed, though a performing version of its first movement prepared by the Beethoven scholar Barry Cooper suggests that a work in heroic mode was being planned, partly in the 'Eroica' key of E flat major, partly in C minor, the key of the Fifth Symphony.

Recordings of the Ninth, like those of Beethoven's other symphonies, have moved on from the time when big, momentous performances of this work, with someone like Leonard Bernstein on the rostrum, were considered *de rigueur*. Most conductors now clip as much as ten minutes off the old-established playing time which, in the days of LP records, meant that performances generally required two discs. Today, the work comfortably fits a single CD, sometimes with space to spare. Even Wilhelm Furtwangler's post-war recordings from Bayreuth and elsewhere, one of them almost eighty minutes long, are thus accommodated. Those who like the Ninth Symphony to sound Meaningful with a capital 'M' still have sufficient recordings to choose from, with stirring performances from Karajan, Barenboim, Boehm and others.

But those who believe the work's interests to be better served by performances lighter, fleeter, more direct and less heroic are equally pampered, particularly by Nikolaus Harnoncourt with the Chamber Orchestra of Europe and Arnold Schoenberg Choir, who know that the work's message is not dependent on portentous delivery. Harnoncourt's is a 'natural' Ninth, if such a thing can be imagined at this stage in the work's history; but this does not mean that it is unexciting or insufficiently universal. On the contrary, it is a riveting performance, every note of which seems to have been examined afresh and illuminated from within, the whole effect alive, vividly textured, never hectoring. In the finale, Robert Holl is a bass soloist who does not boom, the rest of the solo quartet a model of integration (Teldec 0927 46736-2).

Harnoncourt's is a performance on modern instruments, with authentic features. Whether period instruments should play the Ninth Symphony is a matter much disputed; but there is one recording which, in terms of authenticity, is in a class of its own. This is the performance by Philippe Herreweghe, who, with his Orchestre des Champs-Elysées, attempts to suggest what the work should have sounded like in May 1824. Though the sound is deliberately raucous, the results are enthralling, and the swing of the scherzo is like nothing else you will ever have heard (Harmonia Mundi HMC 901687).

Twenty

1826
STRING QUARTET IN B FLAT MAJOR, OP. 130; AND *GROSSE FUGE*, OP. 133

Adagio ma non troppo – Allegro   Presto

Andante con moto, ma non troppo   Alla danza tedesca (Allegro assai)

Cavatina (Adagio molto espressivo)

Finale: *Grosse Fuge* (or) Finale: Allegro vivace

On being told by a friend that this was the greatest of his string quartets, Beethoven answered: 'Each in its own way. Art demands of us that we shall not stand still. You will find a new manner of part-writing and, thank God, there is less lack of fancy than ever before.'

Opus 130 was one of three quartets commissioned from Beethoven in 1822 by his distinguished Russian patron, Prince Galitzin (the others being the E flat major, Op. 127, and the A minor, Op. 132). After considerable delay – caused by the need to complete such trifles as the Ninth Symphony, the *Missa Solemnis* and the *Diabelli* variations – he wrote it in 1825, originally intending its finale to be the mammoth movement destined to have a separate existence under the title of *Grosse Fuge*. Fearing this to be too taxing and incomprehensible to form the climax of an already large work, Beethoven's publishers persuaded him to provide a lighter, shorter finale, which soon established itself as the quartet's 'authorised' ending.

The fugue, ejected from the quartet, survived to become a piece in its own right with its own opus number (Op. 133). Though Beethoven declined to attend its first performance, exclaiming 'Cattle!' and 'Asses!' when told that the audience had failed to demand its instant repetition, his willingness to fit the quartet with a substitute finale suggested that he was fully aware how formidable the fugue actually was. Although, as a separate entity, it remained little easier to perform, players gradually began to accept the challenge. Today, thanks to the expertise of modern performers, the *Grosse Fuge* has regained its lost position. A choice can be made between either finale, each of them equally valid, each of them altering the work's centre of gravity, each of them with points for and against.

Of the work's other five movements, the first begins with all the abrupt changes of speed, mood, volume, rhythm and key that are a special feature of Beethoven's late quartets. Terse little motifs, rather than fully fledged themes, are the material from which the music is constructed, adding to its mood of restlessness; and much use is made of fast scales and arpeggios which, in Beethoven's hands, become intensely dramatic. Material from the slow introduction keeps recurring, contributing to the kaleidoscopic impression of the movement as a whole; but the closing bars, when they come, prove not at all complex – their very simplicity, indeed, is what makes them sublime.

Though famed for their length, these late Beethoven quartets contain movements that are often startlingly short – it's just that there are more of them than quartet tradition dictated. Thus the second movement of Opus 130 is a tiny scherzo in B flat minor – soft, mysterious, wispy, fluttery – with a louder, more rollicking central section in the major. It is followed by the first of two slow movements, launched by a flowing theme on the viola, repeated by the first violin, over a staccato cello accompaniment. Other themes are added in the course of this leisurely music, all of them in keeping with the fine detail of the opening notes.

Between this and the next slow movement comes a graceful 'German' dance, a scherzo-like intermezzo with a gentle offbeat rhythm and lots of running semiquavers, immensely pretty in effect and not at all the sort of thing people tend to associate with the term 'late Beethoven'. But, quite apart from its charm, its presence here is a strategy explained by the succeeding cavatina – a movement which, while also quite short, carries an emotional charge powerful enough to have made Beethoven call it the most moving music he had ever written ('even the remembrance of the emotions it aroused always costs me a tear').

Though only sixty-six bars long, it has a slow intensity that places it, in musical terminology, outside normal metric time. The extraordinary central section – which Beethoven marked *beklemmt* ('oppressed') and in which the first violin deliberately diverges from the throbbing beat of the accompaniment – adds to the music's profoundly grief-stricken effect. Not until Mahler wrote the finale of his First Symphony did a composer bare his soul melodically in quite this way.

In most performances, the cavatina forms the climax of Opus 130, leading to the light relief of the witty rondo finale that Beethoven wrote in place of the *Grosse Fuge*. But when, as now frequently happens, the great fugue is reinstalled in its original position, the balance of the work is altered appreciably. This massive buttress, growing out of a four-note motif with which Beethoven became obsessed while writing these last quartets, is almost a fifteen-minute quartet in itself and has often been treated as such. Preserving a classical layout, Beethoven here compressed four recognisable movements into one.

So there is an 'overture' – really five tiny disjointed overtures, each of them just a handful of notes – out of which, after the first violin has played the four-note motif in bare notes, the fugue springs with a relentlessly violent, jerky counter-subject. The succeeding 'slow movement' is quieter and more flowing, but nervous energy erupts again in a sort of scherzo where the motif is now heard in a context of trills, employed as a source of power rather than decoration. From here, the music becomes increasingly fragmented, and quicker in its changes of mood, as it moves towards its close. But, before that point is reached, Beethoven incorporates one special moment of peace when the first violin takes the four-note motif to the top of its register and sustains it in longer notes.

Modern recordings of Opus 130 generally seize the challenge of incorporating the *Grosse Fuge*, often adding the substitute finale as an appendix, so that listeners can choose their own version. New York's Juilliard Quartet does this in an exemplary recording which adds a further bonus in the form of Beethoven's last quartet, the very different F major, Op. 135. The composer's apparently fatalistic comment on the opening notes of the finale – 'Must it be? It must be' – has prompted many people to assume he was aware that this was to be his last quartet. Yet the nature of the music suggests nothing of the kind. As Hans Keller, never more astute than when writing about string quartets, once pointed out, the music sounds more like the start of a new phase (or late-late period) in Beethoven's output than a final summing-up.

The Juilliard's keen response to every aspect of this terse yet many-sided work adds weight to Keller's comment. Both works incorporate important repeated sections often omitted by other ensembles (Sony SK 62792). As an alternative, the Juilliard's three-disc bargain-price box of all five late quartets, plus the fugue, is equally recommended (SB3K89897), as is the Vegh Quartet's eight-disc *intégrale* of all the works, somewhat bass-heavy and, in the upper register, rather frail, but in all other respects an extraordinary, gripping, deeply private experience (Naïve V 4871 AD 285).

NOTES ON BEETHOVEN

Though Beethoven in his last years remained the greatest, most progressive composer of his time, he feared himself to be a spent force – decrepit, no longer part of Vienna's musical life, a reclusive, shadowy figure from the past. Yet, by today's standards, he was not an old man. Indeed, we would consider him to be mentally still in his prime, even if he was in increasing physical disrepair. To a critic from Leipzig, however, he complained bitterly that nobody performed him any more.

To some extent, his grumbles were justified. Deafness had isolated him, making him feel unwanted. Yet, when he died during a storm in March 1827, having typically raised his fist at the thunderclaps, 20,000 people filled the square outside his lodgings. His funeral was an event. A grand oration by Franz Grillparzer, the Austrian dramatic poet, was read at the cemetery gates. Beethoven may have feared neglect; but his fears were unfounded. His music loomed over Schubert, Mendelssohn, Schumann, Brahms, Berlioz, Wagner, Verdi (who slept with the quartets by his bedside), Tippett and many others, influencing them, inspiring them, challenging them. Even those who reacted against him were paying him tribute of a special kind.

FURTHER READING

Barry Cooper, *Beethoven* (Oxford, 2000)

Placing the man in the context of the music, this is a thoroughly up-to-date study by a leading British Beethoven scholar who has produced a performing version of the unfinished Tenth Symphony.

Martin Cooper, *Beethoven: The Last Decade, 1817–1827* (Oxford, revised 1985)

Absorbing investigation of all aspects of a key period in the composer's life, plus a special section on his death.

Joseph Kerman, *The Beethoven Quartets* (Oxford, 1966)

A comprehensive, not too dauntingly didactic American study of a key portion of Beethoven's output, filled with astute observations. By the author of the controversial *Opera as Drama*.

NOTES ON BEETHOVEN

Lewis Lockwood, *Beethoven* (Norton, 2003)

The latest large-scale biography. Thoughtfully and sensitively written, it is a worthy successor to Solomon, with fresh things to say about whether or not dividing Beethoven's career into three periods has been good for the man and his music.

Charles Rosen, *Beethoven's Piano Sonatas* (Yale, 2002)

Insider's view of the music by a distinguished American concert pianist and authority on classical and romantic style. The sonatas are examined one by one, but the introductory essays on tempo, phrasing, pedalling and kindred topics are no less fascinating.

Maynard Solomon, *Beethoven* (Cassell, 1977; Schirmer, 1998)

The one modern biography that really matters. Placing the music in the context of the man, it tackles such controversial topics as the lure of Paris and what Beethoven really felt about Napoleon. The identity of the Immortal Beloved is traced with the tension of a good detective story, the details so meticulously timetabled that it is impossible to disagree with his findings. The whole book is enthrallingly written and filled with insight.

GLOSSARY

Adagio. Italian musical term meaning 'slow', often interpreted as very slow.

Affettuoso. Italian musical term meaning 'with feeling'.

Agitato. Italian musical term meaning 'agitated'.

Allegro. Italian musical term meaning 'light' or 'fast'. But is an 'allegretto' (meaning, literally, 'a little allegro') slower or faster than allegro? The term is usually accepted as meaning slower, but is irritatingly ambiguous.

Andante. Italian musical term meaning 'at walking pace'.

Andantino. Irritatingly ambiguous Italian musical term, usually taken to mean a little faster than andante, but which can also be interpreted as a little slower than andante.

Appassionata. Italian word for 'impassioned'.

Aria. Italian word for 'song' or 'air', performed by a solo singer, particularly in an operatic context.

Arietta. Italian term for a small or light aria. The arietta which forms the second movement of Beethoven's last piano sonata is neither small nor light.

Arpeggio. Split chord, i.e. a chord whose notes are spread in a harplike manner instead of being sounded simultaneously.

Assai. Italian word for 'very'.

Atonality. Absence of key. Term applied to the music of Schoenberg and his successors in which the music is in no set key or, as Schoenberg himself put it, forms a synthesis of all keys.

Baritone. Singer whose voice range lies between that of a tenor and a bass.

Bel canto. Italian term meaning 'beautiful song' or 'beautiful singing', often referring to the fine-spun vocal lines in the operas of Bellini, Donizetti and Rossini.

Cadenza. Solo passage of varying length, particularly in the first movement of a concerto or in a vocal work, enabling the soloist to display his/her technique in an improvisational manner relevant to the work being performed. Beethoven often wrote down his own cadenzas, sometimes giving the performer a choice of two or more. Classical cadenzas traditionally end with a trill, serving as a signal to the conductor and orchestra to get ready to rejoin the soloist.

Canon. Passage in which a melody performed by one instrument or voice is taken up by another before the previous voice has finished.

Cantabile. Italian musical term meaning 'in a singing manner'.

Cantata. A vocal work, often of a religious nature, usually involving solo voices and chorus with orchestra.

Cavatina. A song, or songlike instrumental piece, usually rather slow.

Chamber orchestra. Smallish orchestra, usually of up to about forty players, suitable for performing in surroundings more intimate than a large concert hall. Though chamber orchestras have their own established repertoire, symphony orchestras frequently intrude on it, just as chamber orchestras today increasingly invade the symphony orchestra's territory, often with conspicuous, indeed revelatory, success.

Chromatic. Put simply, a scale which moves in semitones or, in piano terms, one which uses all the black notes as well as the white notes of the keyboard. Chromatic harmony is thus richer than diatonic harmony, which involves only the notes of the normal major or minor scales.

Coda. Italian word for 'tailpiece'. The closing section of a movement, often dramatically expanded by Beethoven.

Con brio. Italian musical term meaning 'with spirit'.

NOTES ON BEETHOVEN

Concerto. In Beethoven's time, a work for solo instrument (or instruments) and orchestra, involving dramatic contrasts and instrumental repartee. Beethoven composed five numbered piano concertos, a violin concerto and a triple concerto for piano, violin and cello, all of them in three movements with a slow movement in the middle.

Con moto. Italian musical term meaning 'with motion'.

Counterpoint. The combination of two or more melodies or musical figures in such a way that they make musical sense.

Dactylic. Metre based on the repetition of one long beat followed by two shorter ones.

Dominant. The fifth note of the scale. For example, the dominant of the scale of C is the note G, which is four notes above C.

Fantasy. A mood piece of some sort, free-ranging and (at least seemingly) improvisational in style. In Bach's day, a fantasy tended to be an elaborate and contrapuntal keyboard piece, often for organ. Later composers responded to this precedent in their own way.

Finale. The concluding movement of a work (e.g. symphony, string quartet, sonata) in several movements.

Fortissimo. Italian word for 'very loud', abbreviated to *ff* in musical terminology.

Fugue. A type of composition, movement or section of a movement involving a given number of instruments or voices which enter separately, at different pitches, in imitation of each other.

Grosse Fuge. German title for 'Great Fugue'.

Hammerklavier. German for 'piano' (literally, 'hammer keyboard'). Beethoven in the course of his career began to prefer German musical terms to traditional Italian ones, drawing attention in this case to the fact that his *Hammerklavier* sonata was a work of quite exceptional size and power. In fact, all his piano sonatas are automatically *Hammerklavier* sonatas. Schumann and Mahler were among composers who later followed Beethoven's precedent in their emphatic use of German terms.

Intégrale. French term for a complete and integrated series of performances of a particular type of work by a single composer, e.g. Beethoven's sonatas or string quartets.

Kapellmeister. German for 'chapel master', i.e. the musical director of a prince's chapel or court. Came to be a derogatory term ('kapellmeisterish') implying dull musical routine.

Larghetto. Italian musical term meaning 'slow and dignified'.

Maestoso. Italian musical term meaning 'majestic'.

Metronome. Mechanical device for marking the number of beats per minute. J. N. Maelzel's perfected version of the metronome dated from 1814. Metronome specifications (e.g. sixty crotchets per minute) are often placed by composers at the start of a piece of music, so as to signify the desired speed. Beethoven's markings, often exceptionally fast, have often been thought to be misleading (through his use of a faulty metronome) but are now given greater credence, particularly by more open-minded conductors of his symphonies.

Minuet. Dance in triple-time, usually employed by Mozart as the second or the third movement of a string quartet, or the third movement of a symphony. The contrasted middle section of a minuet is known as a trio, because there was a tradition for writing it in three-part harmony.

Moderato. Italian musical term meaning 'at moderate speed'.

Molto. Italian word for 'very'.

Mosso. Italian musical term meaning 'animated'.

Non troppo. Italian musical term meaning 'not too much'.

Opera. Music drama or 'sung play', in which the cast sing their roles rather than speak them – though speech is employed in some operas, including, most expressively, Beethoven's *Fidelio*. A vital component of opera is the orchestra, providing far more than a mere accompaniment, with a chorus, large or small, supplying another (though not essential) dramatic dimension. Opera as we know it was born in Italy around 1600, spreading to France, Germany, Austria and other countries, and inspiring many cities to build their own opera houses for its performance.

Overture. Orchestral prelude to an opera. Beethoven composed four overtures for *Fidelio*, as well as various 'concert' overtures designed for separate performances in a concert hall.

Pianissimo. Italian word for 'very soft'. Abbreviated to *pp* in musical terminology.

Piano trio. From Haydn's time onwards, a work usually written for piano, violin and cello.

Pizzicato. Plucked note on a string instrument.

Prestissimo. Italian musical term meaning 'as fast as possible'.

Presto. Italian musical term meaning 'fast', often taken to mean as fast as possible (which would in fact be *prestissimo*).

Quartet. Work for four instruments, or ensemble specialising in the performance of such a work. The art of the string quartet (two violins, viola and cello) was perfected by Haydn, who influenced (and was influenced by) Mozart. The form was developed and expanded by Beethoven, whose sixteen quartets form a major portion of his output.

NOTES ON BEETHOVEN

Rondo form. Italian term for what was traditionally the spirited finale of a symphony, string quartet or sonata. The word refers to the fact that the opening theme or section of the movement keeps recurring, or coming 'round' again, thereby forming an essential part of the music's structure. Slow movements can also be in rondo form.

Scena (pronounced shay-na). Italian word for 'scene'. A self-sufficient dramatic piece, or 'scene', for solo voice with accompaniment, larger than (but resembling) an operatic aria and often falling into several contrasted sections.

Scherzando. In the manner of a scherzo (see below).

Scherzo. Italian word for 'joke'. Title applied by Beethoven, and to a lesser extent by Haydn, to what until then had been a movement in the form of a minuet. In Beethoven's hands, scherzos replaced minuets in symphonies, string quartets, trios and sonatas. They were generally faster, more volatile and often (though not necessarily) humorous.

Semplice. Italian musical term meaning 'simple'.

Sonata. A work consisting of three or four carefully structured movements. A three-movement Mozart sonata usually has a slow movement enclosed between two faster ones.

Sonata form. Term describing the structure of what was usually the first movement of a sonata during Mozart's period and later. Put simply, it consisted of an 'exposition', based on two or more contrasted themes, a 'development' section in which the material already heard is altered, developed, broken up, or tautened in various ways, a 'recapitulation' in which the introductory material is assembled in something like its original form, and a 'coda' or tailpiece, which rounds the music off or brings it to some sort of closing climax.

Soprano. The highest female voice, ranging from middle C upwards.

Sostenuto. Italian musical term meaning 'sustained'.

Staccato. Italian word for 'short and detached'. Opposite of *legato*, meaning smooth. Signified by a dot over the printed note.

String quartet. A work for four string players, traditionally two violins, viola and cello. Haydn perfected the form, to which Mozart, Beethoven and Schubert all made major contributions. A string quartet is also an ensemble which performs string quartets.

Symphony. Form of orchestral work in several movements, usually of an ambitious nature. Much favoured by Haydn (known as the 'father of the symphony'), Mozart, Beethoven and Schubert.

Symphony orchestra. Orchestra designed to perform symphonies and similar works, with enough players to meet the music's demands. Though Haydn and Mozart visualised the use of big orchestras, their works are elucidated more satisfactorily by small ones, now known as chamber orchestras. The development in the size and firepower of the symphony orchestra took place in the nineteenth century, partly through the extra instruments required by Beethoven's Fifth and Ninth symphonies and the music's dramatic demands. But size is not everything, and the sound of the 'Eroica' symphony played by a chamber orchestra in a smallish hall can be more startling than that of the same work played by a big orchestra in larger surroundings.

Tedesca. Italian word for 'German'. Thus 'danza tedesca' means 'German dance'.

Tenor. High male voice, employed by Mozart in his operas and choral works.

Tonic. The keynote of a scale. For example, the keynote of the scale of C is the note C.

Tremolo. Italian word for 'trembling'. The rapid 'trembling' repetition of a single note, or alternation between two notes.

Trill. Musical term for the rapid alternation of the written note and the note above. Trills are traditionally decorative, but in keyboard terms they are a way of sustaining the sound of a note. Beethoven, particularly in his late works, took the trill out of the field of decoration altogether and employed it to powerful expressive effect (see also **Cadenza**).

Trio. A word with several musical meanings: (1) a work for three instruments, (2) the ensemble which performs such a work, and (3) the name of the middle section of a minuet or scherzo, so called because at one time it was written in three-part harmony. Beethoven's trios were principally for piano, violin and cello, a format which he perfected and which are generally known as piano trios. He also wrote trios for violin, viola and cello (string trios). Ensembles specialising in the performance of trios include the Beaux Arts Trio and the Florestan Trio, both with piano.

Triple concerto. Concerto with three solo instruments. Beethoven's Triple Concerto is for piano, violin and cello with orchestra.

Triplet. A group of three notes of equal duration, written where some other quantity of notes (perhaps just a single note) is implied by the time signature.

Vibrato. Italian word for the rapid vibration in pitch produced by instrumentalists or singers in their performance of a piece of music. Exaggerated vibrato is often described, disparagingly, as 'wobble'. As the history of the symphony orchestra progressed during the twentieth century, so the use of vibrato increased. But, in Beethoven's day and before, orchestral vibrato was not an issue. Performances were vibrato-less, and today many specialist players and orchestras have been learning, with greater and greater success, how to recreate the original sound.

Though some listeners regret the loss of a warm bath of vibrato-laden string tone, the compensations in terms of incisiveness and authenticity are manifest. Besides, vibrato-lovers continue to be lavishly catered for by symphony orchestras which perform in the old familiar way.

Vivace. Italian word for 'lively'.